WHO ARE YOU WALKING LIKE?

AS YOU WALK IN A WORLD OF CONFUSION

VANESSA PRATT

Author's Tranquility Press
ATLANTA, GEORGIA

Copyright © 2023 by VANESSA PRATT

All rights reserved. No part of this publication may be reproduced, distributed or transmitted in any form or by any means, including photocopying, recording, or other electronic or mechanical methods, without the prior written permission of the publisher, except in the case of brief quotations embodied in critical reviews and certain other noncommercial uses permitted by copyright law. For permission requests, write to the publisher, addressed "Attention: Permissions Coordinator," at the address below.

VANESSA PRATT/Author's Tranquility Press
3800 Camp Creek Pkwy SW Bldg. 1400-116 #1255
Atlanta, GA 30331, USA
www.authorstranquilitypress.com

Ordering Information:
Quantity sales. Special discounts are available on quantity purchases by corporations, associations, and others. For details, contact the "Special Sales Department" at the address above.

WHO ARE YOU WALKING LIKE?/VANESSA PRATT
Hardback: 978-1-961123-12-0
Paperback: 978-1-960675-31-6
eBook: 978-1-960675-32-3

Contents

Chapter 1   MISINTERPRETATION OF GOD 1

Chapter 2   GOD CAN USE ANYONE 7

Chapter 3   HONEY DON'T FORGET YOUR ROOTS 13

Chapter 4   LASTING BLESSING 19

Chapter 5   WRITE MY INSIGHTS ON YOUR HEART 25

Chapter 6   INFLAMED WITH PASSION 33

Chapter 7   DON'T DESPISE OTHER'S WEALTH 39

Chapter 8   MY LIPS DETEST WICKEDNESS 45

Chapter 9   IF YOU ARE WISE, YOUR WISDOM WILL REWARD YOU 51

Chapter 10   GOD'S UNSEEN PROVIDENCE 57

Chapter 11   THE PROCESS OF CLEANSING FOR CHRISTIAN LIVING 63

Chapter 12   HONEY, DON'T USE YOUR TONGUE RECKLESSLY 69

Chapter 13   THE PREREQUISITES OF GOD'S WILL 75

Chapter 14   WALKING IN GOD'S PATH 81

Chapter 15   BE A TREE OF LIFE 87

Chapter 16   DO YOU LIVE IN PEACE 93

Chapter 17   LOVE IN UNITY 99

Chapter 18   ALLOW GOD TO FIND AND SEND YOUR HUSBAND TO YOU 105

Chapter 19   GOD RESUME OF GOD'S QUALIFICATIONS 113

Chapter 20   YOU CAN'T KNOW THE WAY WITHOUT GOD 119

Chapter 21	REMEMBER HIS GRACE GUARD YOUR TONGUE	125
Chapter 22	ADVERSITY COMING, BUT GOD CAN PREVAIL	131
Chapter 23	DON'T TRY TO HELP GOD OUT	139
Chapter 24	WITH GOD'S WISDOM, UNDERSTANDING WILL FOLLOW	147
Chapter 25	DON'T SEEK GOD'S BLESSING ON YOUR PLANS	153
Chapter 26	ACCEPTING GOD'S RULES FOR LIVING	161
Chapter 27	LORD, TEACH ME HOW TO BE A LIFE GIVER	167
Chapter 28	LORD I JUST WANT TO STAY IN YOUR PRESENCE	177
Chapter 29	DON'T BE LIKE JEZEBEL'S TRAGEDY	183
Chapter 30	ARE YOU MODELING YOUR RUBIES	191
Chapter 31	LASTING INFLUENCES OF A NOBLE CHARACTER	197

Lifting your Husband through Prayer 201

THE OPTION IS YOURS! 205

God's Beatitudes 208

A Letter from Satan 209

Satan's Beatitudes 210

Women 211

The Four Different Personality Styles................................212

DEDICATION

I dedicate this book to my husband Zachary Pratt, my mother Charlie Mae Thomas, my daughter Evanna, my stepsons Tyrone and Tyrias. Alone with all of my grandchildren to my church family Friendship Baptist Church Duluth, GA. With much love and appreciation.

Acknowledgments

I am truly very grateful to my church Friendship Baptist Church for being a Bible preaching church and Pastor Ronald L. Bowens for his teaching, that comes to my mind while writing this book.

Thanks to other family members and friends for encouragement, support and love. Again I thank you, and I thank God for all of you.

© *Vanessa Pratt*

Preface

As you read the verses in the book of Proverbs when the Lord speaks of His Wisdom, He refers to a **"She"**, not in the feminist sense, but He speaks of His Wisdom with a heartfelt massage. As a woman so often, you know how you can feel things in your heart even before you can see them. Well, the Lord would love for us to feel the passion of His Wisdom is the same way. He loves to share with His people so much that He gave His Only Begotten Son (John 3:16). Whether you are a new or mature Christian, this book will inspire and serve as a reminder of your commitment that we need to live daily in our Bible, "The Word of God." This book will help teach us by looking at the characters of other women, past and present, as they walk through the issues of life.

My Goal as an Author

I truly would like this devotional study information to strengthen your commitment to our Lord and Savior Jesus Christ.

I would love for you to consider walking in faith with Jesus Christ and experience the changes He can and will make in you and through you.

I would love for you to not only develop an understanding of God's Word through developing a commitment to your Bible but, also read this devotional book to grow in the Word of God.

Learn to listen to the voice of God and what He has to say about you going forward in His Will, being fruitful to increase the number of new Christians as you assist with subduing the earth and doing the will of God for Him to be praised and glorified.

Life After the Ventilator

If you cannot breathe on your own because infection or an injury has caused your lungs to fail, you may need a ventilator.

A ventilator is a medical device that provides oxygen through a breathing tube to the lungs, taking over the body's breathing process. This gives the patient time to heal and recover from a serious illness.

Yes, I was on a ventilator for five days on September 10, 2020 and an additional two more days stay in the hospital after that. Let me share my story in hopes you never find yourself in this predicament.

My husband Zack and I had taken a weekend trip to Florida to visit our sons and granddaughters for the Labor Day weekend. We had a great time visiting with the grandbabies and spending one night a piece at each son's home. While there, one of the sons had cooked some ribs alone with all the sides and after eating the ribs, one of my teeth had chipped on a bone. So after our return home I made an appointment for Wednesday with a new dentist who was recommended by a coworker as their costs for the temporary crowns was a lot less expensive than my regular dentist. That night after I came home from the dentist, I noticed my weekly medicine had run out as well as Zack's. So I refilled our containers and we took our meds and turned in for the night.

The next day, I went to work. I kept a small mirror on my desk to make sure nothing was on my face. I just happened to glance in the mirror when I noticed my lip was swollen and thought it was from the dental work I had done. I began to feel a little strange and then I noticed my lip had dropped and my face begun to swell, too. I informed my boss that I needed to get to the hospital to see what was going on. As I was driving myself to the hospital, I called the dentist office thinking I was having a reaction from the numbing medicine they used. I drove myself to the emergency room of the nearest hospital because I didn't think I would be able to make it okay to my doctor's office, and I truly thank God I got there without an accident or an incident.

    I called my husband while in the waiting room telling him there was no need for him to come over to the hospital as he would not be allowed in because of the COVID situation and that I would be home in a few hours. While in the emergency room, I asked the doctor if I could remove my mask so that he could see what was going on with my face and that was the last thing I remembered. Those hours turned into days. The doctor found Zack's number in my phone and called him to inform him that they needed to put a pick line in me and place me on a ventilator. Five days later as they removed me from that ventilator all I kept hearing was code red and code blue all night I tried to turn my body to see if the nurses were still in the hall or if I was absent from the body and present with the Lord.

PROVERBS 1

1. The proverbs of Solomon the son of David, king of Israel;
2. To know wisdom and instruction; to perceive the words of understanding;
3. To receive the instruction of wisdom, justice, and judgment, and equity;
4. To give subtilty to the simple, to the young man knowledge and discretion.
5. A wise man will hear, and will increase learning; and a man of understanding shall attain unto wise counsels:
6. To understand a proverb, and the interpretation; the words of the wise, and their dark sayings.
7. The fear of the LORD is the beginning of knowledge: but fools despise wisdom and instruction.
8. My son, hear the instruction of thy father, and forsake not the law of thy mother:
9. For they shall be an ornament of grace unto thy head, and chains about thy neck.
10. My son, if sinners entice thee, consent thou not.
11. If they say, Come with us, let us lay wait for blood, let us lurk privily for the innocent without cause:
12. Let us swallow them up alive as the grave; and whole, as those that go down into the pit:
13. We shall find all precious substance, we shall fill our houses with spoil:
14. Cast in thy lot among us; let us all have one purse:
15. My son, walk not thou in the way with them; refrain thy foot from their path:
16. For their feet run to evil, and make haste to shed blood.
17. Surely in vain the net is spread in the sight of any bird.

18. *And they lay wait for their own blood; they lurk privily for their own lives.*
19. *So are the ways of every one that is greedy of gain; which taketh away the life of the owners thereof.*
20. *Wisdom crieth without; she uttereth her voice in the streets:*
21. *She crieth in the chief place of concourse, in the openings of the gates: in the city she uttereth her words, saying,*
22. *How long, ye simple ones, will ye love simplicity? and the scorners delight in their scorning, and fools hate knowledge?*
23. *Turn you at my reproof: behold, I will pour out my spirit unto you, I will make known my words unto you.*
24. *Because I have called, and ye refused; I have stretched out my hand, and no man regarded;*
25. *But ye have set at nought all my counsel, and would none of my reproof:*
26. *I also will laugh at your calamity; I will mock when your fear cometh;*
27. *When your fear cometh as desolation, and your destruction cometh as a whirlwind; when distress and anguish cometh upon you.*
28. *Then shall they call upon me, but I will not answer; they shall seek me early, but they shall not find me:*
29. *For that they hated knowledge, and did not choose the fear of the LORD:*
30. *They would none of my counsel: they despised all my reproof.*
31. *Therefore shall they eat of the fruit of their own way, and be filled with their own devices.*
32. *For the turning away of the simple shall slay them, and the prosperity of fools shall destroy them.*

But whoso hearkeneth unto me shall dwell safely, and shall be quiet from fear of evil.

Chapter 1

MISINTERPRETATION OF GOD

The fear of the LORD is the beginning of knowledge: but fools despise wisdom and instruction.

Proverbs 1:7

Growing-up the only time I attended church was when I spent time with my grandparents or when they were able to come to pick me up to spend time at their house. Nothing is more important than what we believe or know about God. It determines how we perceive ourselves, also how we view our relationships with others, it can also define what we understand and interpret as our view of God. As a young child, I would ask my father about God because I did not understand that two spirits were operating in this world, the Spirit of God (light), and the spirit of Satan (darkness). Since my parents didn't attend church at that time or understand who they were born in the likeness of, we had a bunch of uncertainty at home. My father would come home drunk most of the time, fighting and swearing, and my mother had a dominate personality often with my dad, so that didn't help matters at home. Often, we had to call the police out to our home for domestic abuse issues.

One thing for sure our household truly didn't have was the presence of God anywhere in our home. After I was about seven or eight years old, I began to ask my father who is God and he would tell me that, there was no God. As you can see, we had a lot of foolish thinking that existed and a big misunderstanding about God in our home. If we had a Bible and did Bible study alone with going to church, maybe then we would have known God's Word as our **"Basic Instruction Before Leaving Earth."** I thank God for continuing to open my heart and making me feel that something was missing. I grew up and started going to church for myself. God placed me in a church that encouraged and developed me, in the Word of God with training classes, conferences, and leadership events. He built me up as I began to seek His Word and wisdom. As my parents continue to see God raising me in the Spirit of the Lord, the Lord led me to write a book called "Under His Cleaning for Christian Living." My parents then started going to church and they gave their lives to the Lord. I thank God that before my father passed away, he came to know the Lord as his Savior.

God showed me what was missing in my life. He showed me that I needed to know Him personally, to be born again, born into the spirit of Jesus Christ, so the Holy Spirit could come in and take up residence in my heart. I could not own Him without fellowshipping with Him all the time, not now and then, but I had to be in daily fellowship. I need to read my Bible and have a church home so I can learn from the preacher and others if, what I am hearing is correct and it's the Word of God. Also, seek to live according to His Word and standards so He can be glorified in my character. Finally, learning that I can't forsake the fellowship of my Christian brothers and sisters in Jesus Christ. How would I ever truly know how Christians should conduct themselves and know the Word of God for myself?

Everyone needs change in their life. A few things that I've asked the Lord to help me change are: first, I need God to make me better every day. I need His character to shine out of me, I need Him for His personality and daily actions the Father desires of me. I need Him to evaluate me as I try to get an accurate picture of my walk as a Christian and a light for Jesus Christ. Every day as a Christian there's something within me that I need to grow up more in the likeness of Jesus Christ. I can't be "offended" because of the things people say or do around me in this world because the world does not care who it offends and more importantly if they offend Jesus Christ, I can't think that I am above being offended. As I continue getting older and going through life, I've seen how people have attempted to remove any image or memory of God and Christianity from society. They have made us remove God from schools, work, the government, and everything else. They also ask people not to speak about God in public places in hopes of not "offending" others. But Jesus Christ gave us **The Great Commission** to spread the Word of God around the world. Also, to share that this world is not our home. How can we allow God to be removed from our society it will leave us without any values or looking like we are the character and light of this world for Jesus Christ. I know I have gotten off my topic a little but, what we need to realize is that all the changes we want to be done in us and around us have a starting point. It starts within you. But you have to allow God to work in you, so He can use you to start the outward work within the world. You must seek God first and then allow Him to put the rest of the puzzle together.

ACTION STEPS:

* Seek to learn the **"Basic Instruction Before Leaving Earth"** (**Bible**) so you may know the ways of God.
* God is more than willing to pour out His heart and make known His thoughts to you.
* How are you seeking to walk? In the ways of God Or the ways of your flesh?

THOUGHT FOR THE DAY:

Wisdom is the mind of God revealed to you by reading His Word. In Proverbs through Solomon, God seeks to help us understand that a fool is not someone with a mental deficiency but someone with a character deficiency such as rebellion, laziness, or anger. The fool is not stupid but is unable to tell right from wrong, good from bad, or have the heart to seek understanding of God's Word.

PRAYER:

Lord, forgive me for seeking to walk in the path of foolishness and forsaking God's Word. Help me learn of Your Ways and Wisdom. In the name of Jesus, I pray. Amen.

PROVERBS 2

1. My son, if thou wilt receive my words, and hide my commandments with thee;
2. So that thou incline thine ear unto wisdom, and apply thine heart to understanding;
3. Yea, if thou criest after knowledge, and liftest up thy voice for understanding;
4. If thou seekest her as silver, and searchest for her as for hid treasures;
5. Then shalt thou understand the fear of the LORD, and find the knowledge of God.
6. For the LORD giveth wisdom: out of his mouth cometh knowledge and understanding.
7. He layeth up sound wisdom for the righteous: he is a buckler to them that walk uprightly.
8. He keepeth the paths of judgment, and preserveth the way of his saints.
9. Then shalt thou understand righteousness, and judgment, and equity; yea, every good path.
10. When wisdom entereth into thine heart, and knowledge is pleasant unto thy soul;
11. Discretion shall preserve thee, understanding shall keep thee:
12. To deliver thee from the way of the evil man, from the man that speaketh froward things;
13. Who leave the paths of uprightness, to walk in the ways of darkness;
14. Who rejoice to do evil, and delight in the frowardness of the wicked;
15. Whose ways are crooked, and they froward in their paths:

16. *To deliver thee from the strange woman, even from the stranger which flattereth with her words;*
17. *Which forsaketh the guide of her youth, and forgetteth the covenant of her God.*
18. *For her house inclineth unto death, and her paths unto the dead.*
19. *None that go unto her return again, neither take they hold of the paths of life.*
20. *That thou mayest walk in the way of good men, and keep the paths of the righteous.*
21. *For the upright shall dwell in the land, and the perfect shall remain in it.*
22. *But the wicked shall be cut off from the earth, and the transgressors shall be rooted out of it.*

Chapter 2

GOD CAN USE ANYONE

For the LORD giveth wisdom: out of his mouth cometh knowledge and understanding.

Proverbs 2:6

Today's individuals, both young and old feel as if they don't have to listen to anyone for advice to assist with any kind of direction or standards of living. We truly do not understand how God has given us benefits when we seek His moral standards of living. When we look at the book of Judges, we can see that God not only used men, but He also used a woman, Deborah. Also, Deborah is introduced as a prophetess, the wife of Lapidoth, Judges 4:4. God chose men and women to communicate His will to His people. Deborah was truly used as a great woman of God to not only lead her community but also to lead the men into war. The first thing we learn from Deborah is that she had a special relationship with God. She was called by Him and commissioned to speak in His name. All of Israel recognized that special relationship. In the words of Deborah's song, she was one who loved God, and as a result, was "like the sun when it comes out in full strength" (Judges 5:31). Second, Deborah was not a military leader, when she was about to call on her people to fight the Canaanites of Hazor, she first summoned Barak, a military man, in the name of the Lord. She then passed on the instructions from God, which Barak was to follow. We can conclude from this that God did not want Deborah in the role of a military leader, but God had appointed Deborah as prophetess and judge and had communicated His intention to commission Barak to lead the battle.

Deborah's confidence was rooted in a close and personal relationship with God and her awareness that God had chosen to use her to guide His people. She could do more than judge and prophesy. She could stir up the people. This noble woman must have had a sparkling personality and surely, a dauntless spirit. She could inspire others with the same trust in God that she had. She became great because she saw a need and did something about it. She said, "The rulers ceased in Israel until I Deborah arose . . . a mother in Israel." And she mothered her people well, the land had rested for forty years. In displaying these qualities Deborah stands as a timeless example for spiritual leaders, also, she helps us to understand clearly that we must trust in the Lord with our heart and to lean not unto our understanding, and in all of our ways we should acknowledge Him.

Deborah reminds us that God gifts whomever, is willing to be used for spiritual leadership. At the same time, God's choosing Barak as the military commander may indicate that not every leadership role is appropriate for women.

Deborah was a woman who balanced her many roles in life. She was a wife, a prophetess, and a judge. In each capacity the Lord gave her, she served Him competently. It is not always easy to balance our roles in life. Let's be sure that we seek God's guidance and like Deborah, serve Him in each of our callings.

We must make sure that as godly women we have an opportunity to exercise the gifts given to us by the Holy Spirit.

ACTION STEPS:

- God promises to guide those who obey and trust Him.
- Those who obey must actively explore God's Word.
- Depend on God in every part of your life. And He will guide, protect and comfort you.

THOUGHT FOR THE DAY:

No matter where life leads anyone if you are willing to trust God with your heart and lean not unto your understanding, He can use you to be a great leader, teacher, singer, preacher and the list go, on and on, for the glory of His Kingdom.

Ask God to reveal Himself to you so that you may love Him and obey Him.

PRAYER:

Lord, help me to know you and trust you with my heart so I may learn not to lean on my own understanding as I acknowledge you in all of my ways daily. In the name of Jesus, I pray. Amen.

PROVERBS 3

1. *My son, forget not my law; but let thine heart keep my commandments:*
2. *For length of days, and long life, and peace, shall they add to thee.*
3. *Let not mercy and truth forsake thee: bind them about thy neck; write them upon the table of thine heart:*
4. *So shalt thou find favour and good understanding in the sight of God and man.*
5. *Trust in the LORD with all thine heart; and lean not unto thine own understanding.*
6. *In all thy ways acknowledge him, and he shall direct thy paths.*
7. *Be not wise in thine own eyes: fear the LORD, and depart from evil.*
8. *It shall be health to thy navel, and marrow to thy bones.*
9. *Honour the LORD with thy substance, and with the first fruits of all thine increase:*
10. *So shall thy barns be filled with plenty, and thy presses shall burst out with new wine.*
11. *My son, despise not the chastening of the LORD; neither be weary of his correction:*
12. *For whom the LORD loveth he correcteth; even as a father the son in whom he delighteth.*
13. *Happy is the man that findeth wisdom, and the man that getteth understanding.*
14. *For the merchandise of it is better than the merchandise of silver, and the gain thereof than fine gold.*
15. *She is more precious than rubies: and all the things thou canst desire are not to be compared unto her.*

16. Length of days is in her right hand; and in her left hand riches and honour.
17. Her ways are ways of pleasantness, and all her paths are peace.
18. She is a tree of life to them that lay hold upon her: and happy is every one that retaineth her.
19. The LORD by wisdom hath founded the earth; by understanding hath he established the heavens.
20. By his knowledge the depths are broken up, and the clouds drop down the dew.
21. My son, let not them depart from thine eyes: keep sound wisdom and discretion:
22. So shall they be life unto thy soul, and grace to thy neck.
23. Then shalt thou walk in thy way safely, and thy foot shall not stumble.
24. When thou liest down, thou shalt not be afraid: yea, thou shalt lie down, and thy sleep shall be sweet.
25. Be not afraid of sudden fear, neither of the desolation of the wicked, when it cometh.
26. For the LORD shall be thy confidence, and shall keep thy foot from being taken.
27. Withhold not good from them to whom it is due, when it is in the power of thine hand to do it.
28. Say not unto thy neighbour, Go, and come again, and tomorrow I will give; when thou hast it by thee.
29. Devise not evil against thy neighbour, seeing he dwelleth securely by thee.
30. Strive not with a man without cause, if he have done thee no harm.
31. Envy thou not the oppressor, and choose none of his ways.
32. For the froward is abomination to the LORD: but his secret is with the righteous.

33. *The curse of the LORD is in the house of the wicked: but he blesseth the habitation of the just.*
34. *Surely he scorneth the scorners: but he giveth grace unto the lowly.*
35. *The wise shall inherit glory: but shame shall be the promotion of fools.*

Chapter 3

HONEY DON'T FORGET YOUR ROOTS

My son, forget not my law; but let thine heart keep my commandments.

Proverbs 3:1

Samson had fought and killed hundreds of Philistines because of his great physical strength, a gift from God. No Philistine force had been able to overtake him. But Samson was morally weak, a victim of his passion for women outside of his race, religion, and his family values. When Samson began an affair with a woman named Delilah the Philistines saw an opportunity to learn the secret of Samson's strength. They offer her a fortune to discover the secret of Samson's strength and betray it to them. Delilah, eager to gain the promised wealth, and fame, complied.

At first, Samson put Delilah off with lies, telling her that fresh thongs or new ropes or braiding his hair would weaken him. Three times as Samson slept, Delilah tried him, and then awakened him with her crying that the Philistines were upon him. Each time Samson easily broke free, ready to fight. But with each fresh lie Delilah complained, insisting that if Samson truly loved her, he would confide in her. Finally, Samson gave in to her nagging and told her the truth. The secret of his strength lay in the fact that as a Nazirite his braided hair had never been cut.

The Bible gives us a picture of Delilah. She was a beautiful woman and was very aware of the power her sexuality gave her and quick to use sex for her gain. While Samson had fallen in love with Delilah, she only pretended affection for him. Delilah was more than willing to let Samson use her body because she was using him to become rich (Judges 19).

As you could imagine Samson was so in love with Delilah that he couldn't see what was happening to him. Delilah's repeated efforts to get Samson's secret of his strength seemed so transparent, but Samson was blinded by his passion and was easily manipulated by Delilah. Delilah would pretend that she had a doubt about his love, and would appeal unto him to prove his love by revealing his secret. Finally, it had worn Samson down.

Delilah was determined to get ahead, and chose to use sex to advance herself. Delilah also betrayed herself, because sex is a gift from God to be shared between husband and wife to bind them together in an even deepening commitment to one another. When we engage in sex outside of this context we become as much a victim as the sexual partner. Sexual weakness can bring down even the most powerful people.

ACTION STEPS:

- * Keeping yourself sexually pure and equally yoked protects you from being overpowered by your flesh.
- * Stay in fellowship with the people of God, so you don't become overpowered by things around you.

* Do not conform to this world, but be ye transformed by the renewing of your mind, that you may prove what is the good and perfect will of God.

Romans 12:2

THOUGHT FOR THE DAY:

When you choose to engage in sex outside of marriage, you lose sight of the value God has placed within you as an individual. Ultimately, you are seen by others as nothing more than an object to be used.

Taking a stand against engaging in sex outside Matrimony shows that you are standing for your values and worth because sexual immorality is a form of slavery, people using one another for their gratification with no concern for the other person or themselves. God can use the worst person to accomplish His will and purpose.

PRAYER:

Lord, strengthen me and create in me a clean heart, a heart filled with your love and goodness. Jesus, I need to know You and your ways, because, without You, I am lost and undone. I am nothing apart from You. I want to be perfect and grow in your wisdom and understanding of your ways. In the name of Jesus, I pray. Amen.

PROVERBS 4

1. *Hear, ye children, the instruction of a father, and attend to know understanding.*
2. *For I give you good doctrine, forsake ye not my law.*
3. *For I was my father's son, tender and only beloved in the sight of my mother.*
4. *He taught me also, and said unto me, Let thine heart retain my words: keep my commandments, and live.*
5. *Get wisdom, get understanding: forget it not; neither decline from the words of my mouth.*
6. *Forsake her not, and she shall preserve thee: love her, and she shall keep thee.*
7. *Wisdom is the principal thing; therefore get wisdom: and with all thy getting get understanding.*
8. *Exalt her, and she shall promote thee: she shall bring thee to honour, when thou dost embrace her.*
9. *She shall give to thine head an ornament of grace: a crown of glory shall she deliver to thee.*
10. *Hear, O my son, and receive my sayings; and the years of thy life shall be many.*
11. *I have taught thee in the way of wisdom; I have led thee in right paths.*
12. *When thou goest, thy steps shall not be straitened; and when thou runnest, thou shalt not stumble.*
13. *Take fast hold of instruction; let her not go: keep her; for she is thy life.*
14. *Enter not into the path of the wicked, and go not in the way of evil men.*
15. *Avoid it, pass not by it, turn from it, and pass away.*

16. *For they sleep not, except they have done mischief; and their sleep is taken away, unless they cause some to fall.*
17. *For they eat the bread of wickedness, and drink the wine of violence.*
18. *But the path of the just is as the shining light, that shineth more and more unto the perfect day.*
19. *The way of the wicked is as darkness: they know not at what they stumble.*
20. *My son, attend to my words; incline thine ear unto my sayings.*
21. *Let them not depart from thine eyes; keep them in the midst of thine heart.*
22. *For they are life unto those that find them, and health to all their flesh.*
23. *Keep thy heart with all diligence; for out of it are the issues of life.*
24. *Put away from thee a froward mouth, and perverse lips put far from thee.*
25. *Let thine eyes look right on, and let thine eyelids look straight before thee.*
26. *Ponder the path of thy feet, and let all thy ways be established.*
27. *Turn not to the right hand nor to the left: remove thy foot from evil.*

Chapter 4

LASTING BLESSING

Forsake her not, and she shall preserve thee: love her, and she shall keep thee.

Proverbs 4:6

Ruth's relationship with God began the way most relationships with Him began. Ruth married an Israelite man, one of Naomi's sons. Looking at the life that Naomi mirrored before Ruth, helped Ruth to come to know and value not only the life of Naomi but also the only true and living God that Naomi spoke about. After Naomi's sons passed away, she decided to give them both blessings and tell them to return to Judah. Naomi told them the Lord grant that they may find rest, each in the house of her husband (Ruth 1:9). Naomi truly loved her daughters-in-law and had a great love for God, she became the bridge that passed Ruth over to faith.

Naomi urged the two young women to go home and find new husbands, and Orpah returned. However, Ruth refused to return home. She truly loved her mother-in-law and refuse to desert her. Ruth realized that this decision called for a faith commitment to Naomi's God. Naomi continued to urge Ruth to return home. Ruth then expressed her commitment in unmistakable terms. Ruth told Naomi, "For wherever you go; I will go. And wherever you lodge, I will lodge. Your people shall be my people. And your God, my God. Where you die, I will die. And there will I be buried. The Lord do so to me, and more also, if anything but death parts you and me." (Ruth 1:16-17)

Ruth's commitment to stay with Naomi and the people of Israel, also showed that she was making a commitment to the only true and living God. First, the deep love and appreciation for Naomi was expressed in loyalty. Ruth chose to stay with Naomi rather than go back to her father's home and stay in her own familiar country. She decided to walk into an uncertain future in a strange land.

For Ruth, Judah was a strange land, full of unfamiliar customs. But Ruth knew that in Naomi she truly had a mentor, and she followed her advice. Naomi sent Ruth out to gather grain that the harvesters missed, a process called gleaning. Gleaning was hard work. Ruth would "continue from morning" until late in the day gathering food for Naomi and herself. Ruth's modesty and virtue won the admiration of one of Naomi's relatives. Naomi explained to Ruth the law of the redeeming relative. Naomi urged Ruth to approach the man and ask him to take on the redeeming relative's responsibility.

Ruth allowed herself to be mentored by Naomi in the selection of a husband. Although Naomi's nephew was not young or handsome, Ruth realized that he was a man of quality, and she followed Naomi's advice. In every way, Ruth showed herself to be loyal, hard-working, sensible, and responsive to Naomi's advice. Ruth had a deep respect for Naomi, as well as a real love for her mother-in-law. Long before Boaz met Ruth or knew her by sight, he had heard nothing but good things about her. So, when Boaz first met her, he was able to say, "It has been fully reported to me, all that you have done for your mother-in-law since the death of your husband, and how you have left your father and your mother and the land of your birth, and have come to a people whom you did not know before" (Ruth 2:11). Aware of her qualities, Boaz treated her favorably, he instructed the men not to molest her, and he instructed his harvesters to be sure to leave handfuls of grain for Ruth to collect.

Naomi had learned what was happening, and she also realized that Boaz was a near relative of hers, so she felt that God was opening a door for Ruth. She instructed Ruth to keep working in Boaz's field and after several weeks had passed Naomi took Ruth aside and explained her concern for Ruth's future security. Naomi knew that Boaz was qualified not only to marry Ruth but also to reclaim the lands of Naomi's husband. So, Naomi advised Ruth even down to the way she needed to approach Boaz. Boaz married Ruth and the marriage was blessed with a son, and that son became the grandfather of King David and an ancestor of Jesus Christ.

ACTION STEPS:

- Always be wise enough to seek wisdom from a seasoned saint, it can keep you from a lot of heartaches and pains.
- Always live your life in a way that others recognize you are worth following.
- Although you may feel insignificant, God can use your story to win other souls for His glory.

THOUGHT FOR THE DAY:

Remember that God says a man should find a wife. He said, "He that finds a wife finds a good thing and finds favor in the sight of the Lord." Also, character counts so much more than finding someone that looks good on the outside. Remember that you should be more concerned with a Godly spouse than a sexy one.

PRAYER:

Lord, redeem my desires and make them a pure and holy gift unto you. Send me a spouse, Lord Jesus. I am hungry and thirsty for your righteousness. I do want to be like you, so I may experience the abundant life you came to give me. In the name of Jesus, I pray. Amen.

PROVERBS 5

1. *My son, attend unto my wisdom, and bow thine ear to my understanding:*
2. *That thou mayest regard discretion, and that thy lips may keep knowledge.*
3. *For the lips of a strange woman drop as an honeycomb, and her mouth is smoother than oil:*
4. *But her end is bitter as wormwood, sharp as a two-edged sword.*
5. *Her feet go down to death; her steps take hold on hell.*
6. *Lest thou shouldest ponder the path of life, her ways are moveable, that thou canst not know them.*
7. *Hear me now therefore, O ye children, and depart not from the words of my mouth.*
8. *Remove thy way far from her, and come not nigh the door of her house:*
9. *Lest thou give thine honour unto others, and thy years unto the cruel:*
10. *Lest strangers be filled with thy wealth; and thy labours be in the house of a stranger;*
11. *And thou mourn at the last, when thy flesh and thy body are consumed,*
12. *And say, How have I hated instruction, and my heart despised reproof;*
13. *And have not obeyed the voice of my teachers, nor inclined mine ear to them that instructed me!*
14. *I was almost in all evil in the midst of the congregation and assembly.*
15. *Drink waters out of thine own cistern, and running waters out of thine own well.*

16. *Let thy fountains be dispersed abroad, and rivers of waters in the streets.*
17. *Let them be only thine own, and not strangers' with thee.*
18. *Let thy fountain be blessed: and rejoice with the wife of thy youth.*
19. *Let her be as the loving hind and pleasant roe; let her breasts satisfy thee at all times; and be thou ravished always with her love.*
20. *And why wilt thou, my son, be ravished with a strange woman, and embrace the bosom of a stranger?*
21. *For the ways of man are before the eyes of the LORD, and he pondereth all his goings.*
22. *His own iniquities shall take the wicked himself, and he shall be holden with the cords of his sins.*
23. *He shall die without instruction; and in the greatness of his folly he shall go astray.*

Chapter 5

WRITE MY INSIGHTS ON YOUR HEART

My son, attend unto my wisdom and bow thine ear to my understanding: That thou mayest regard discretion, and that thy lips may keep knowledge.

Proverbs 5:1-2

Yolanda (born Yolanda Yvette Adams, on August 27, 1961) was raised in Houston, Texas. She is the oldest of six siblings. Her house was bathed in music, and along with six other siblings, has had considerable exposure to all types of music: classical, gospel, Motown, as well as other genres. Her family offered her a solid religious upbringing, and as a small child, she created for herself an imaginary friend she called "Hallelujah" and sang a solo in church at age three. She grew up with the classic gospel sounds of James Cleveland and the Edwin Hawkins Singers, but hers was also a musically eclectic household. Adams's mother, a pianist who majored in music in college, introduced her daughter to jazz, classical music, and secular R&B. Adams joined a gospel choir, the Southeast Inspirational Choir, shortly after her father's death when she was 13. After she graduated from college, she continued to perform on weekends.

Yolanda has accomplished what few singers before her have ever achieved: The ability to attract fans from all walks of life without ever straying from the intricate roots that nurtured her Grammy-winning voice in the first place. She is an inspiration to many. This should not come as a surprise because her career spans over 15 impressive years of classical singing. Unlike some contemporary Christian musicians—black and white—who consciously blurred the line between sacred and secular music and described religious feeling with romantic terms such as love and commitment, there's no doubt in her songs whether she has given the religious message.

Yolanda brings her music to a wider audience not by watering down her message, but by making a record of supreme power, conviction, and glorious beauty, incorporating elements of traditional gospel, hip-hop, jazz, and R&B into daring arrangements. She continues to be a blessing with her radio station to her listeners daily as she reveals God's Biblical Scriptures with great passion, for us to live on purpose, with practical truths, warning against reckless words, reckless living, selfishness, dishonesty, unforgiveness, and foolish companions to name a few. She and Minister Anthony Valary provide great principles and eternal truths which should become the core values that govern our lives. They help provide direction and inspiration for everyday challenges that God's people face. Yolanda has a beautiful "darling" daughter Taylor Ayanna. She speaks of her often as she shares the points of power in her biblical inspiration and nuggets from the Word of God. God is truly being glorified in her walk and her life. She has allowed herself to pay attention to God's wisdom, listen to Him, and write God's commandments on her heart to pour into others. Yolanda has truly allowed God to use her not only through her singing but also daily as she gives wisdom and insight into God's Word.

How does one top all that, you may ask? The five-time Grammy Award winner has joined with thirty years of broadcast veteran Brother Larry Jones, comedian Marcus Wiley, and Minister Anthony Valary hosting The Yolanda Adams Morning Show which currently airs on Urban Gospel stations owned by Radio One.

ACTION STEPS:

* Always seek to follow the heart and wisdom of God, and it will bring you His peace, and joy, which will give you an insight and understanding of His Word.
* Never seek other people to approve the work God has given you to do, as they sometimes make you miss listening to and hearing from God.
* Just like "Yolanda Adams" you can also be a Biblical inspiration as you allow God to use you for His glory.

THOUGHT FOR THE DAY:

Remember, you can influence others Biblically by living on purpose from the Word of God if you allow Him to speak to you and through you. Also, walk in a way that others can see God in you and read you as His open book.

PRAYER:

Lord, speak through me and teach me your Biblical truths, so my steps can be ordered in your Word for your glory and the upbuilding of your Kingdom. In the name of Jesus, I pray. Amen.

PROVERBS 6

1. *My son, if thou be surety for thy friend, if thou hast stricken thy hand with a stranger,*
2. *Thou art snared with the words of thy mouth, thou art taken with the words of thy mouth.*
3. *Do this now, my son, and deliver thyself, when thou art come into the hand of thy friend; go, humble thyself, and make sure thy friend.*
4. *Give not sleep to thine eyes, nor slumber to thine eyelids.*
5. *Deliver thyself as a roe from the hand of the hunter, and as a bird from the hand of the fowler.*
6. *Go to the ant, thou sluggard; consider her ways, and be wise:*
7. *Which having no guide, overseer, or ruler,*
8. *Provideth her meat in the summer, and gathereth her food in the harvest.*
9. *How long wilt thou sleep, O sluggard? when wilt thou arise out of thy sleep?*
10. *Yet a little sleep, a little slumber, a little folding of the hands to sleep:*
11. *So shall thy poverty come as one that travelleth, and thy want as an armed man.*
12. *A naughty person, a wicked man, walketh with a froward mouth.*
13. *He winketh with his eyes, he speaketh with his feet, he teacheth with his fingers;*
14. *Frowardness is in his heart, he deviseth mischief continually; he soweth discord.*
15. *Therefore shall his calamity come suddenly; suddenly shall he be broken without remedy.*

16. *These six things doth the LORD hate: yea, seven are an abomination unto him:*
17. *A proud look, a lying tongue, and hands that shed innocent blood,*
18. *An heart that deviseth wicked imaginations, feet that be swift in running to mischief,*
19. *A false witness that speaketh lies, and he that soweth discord among brethren.*
20. *My son, keep thy father's commandment, and forsake not the law of thy mother:*
21. *Bind them continually upon thine heart, and tie them about thy neck.*
22. *When thou goest, it shall lead thee; when thou sleepest, it shall keep thee; and when thou awakest, it shall talk with thee.*
23. *For the commandment is a lamp; and the law is light; and reproofs of instruction are the way of life:*
24. *To keep thee from the evil woman, from the flattery of the tongue of a strange woman.*
25. *Lust not after her beauty in thine heart; neither let her take thee with her eyelids.*
26. *For by means of a whorish woman a man is brought to a piece of bread: and the adultress will hunt for the precious life.*
27. *Can a man take fire in his bosom, and his clothes not be burned?*
28. *Can one go upon hot coals, and his feet not be burned?*
29. *So he that goeth in to his neighbour's wife; whosoever toucheth her shall not be innocent.*
30. *Men do not despise a thief, if he steal to satisfy his soul when he is hungry;*
31. *But if he be found, he shall restore sevenfold; he shall give all the substance of his house.*

32. But whoso committeth adultery with a woman lacketh understanding: he that doeth it destroyeth his own soul.
33. A wound and dishonour shall he get; and his reproach shall not be wiped away.
34. For jealousy is the rage of a man: therefore he will not spare in the day of vengeance.
35. He will not regard any ransom; neither will he rest content, though thou givest many gifts.

Chapter 6

INFLAMED WITH PASSION

When thou goest, it shall lead thee; when thou sleepest, it shall keep thee; and when thou awakest, it shall talk with thee.

Proverbs 6: 22

Bathsheba was married to Uriah, a Hittite who served as an officer in David's army. He was listed among the thirty-seven top-ranking heroes. He was one of David's **"mighty men"** (2 Samuels 23:39). His house was in Jerusalem near the palace and when he was not at war he also served in David's palace as a guard. Bathsheba's looked so good that the Hebrew word used to describe her appearance was "yapeh," which means "good looking" she was so beautiful that when men looked at her, they were aroused and had a desire for her.

Bathsheba was a very beautiful woman. One night when Uriah was away campaigning with the army, David saw Bathsheba bathing in her courtyard, and he was aroused. He sent his servants to get her, had sex with her, and sent her home. Bathsheba became pregnant. Now David had to rethink his adulteress moment, so he called for Bathsheba's husband Uriah to come home, thinking Uriah was going to be ready to sleep with his wife so Bathsheba's pregnancy could be passed off as his. Uriah was feeling so duty-bound to share in the hardship of his army companions that he didn't go into his house to sleep with his wife. David tried to cover up. Now that this plan didn't work, he began to panic and try to rethink what to do next. David sent instructions to his commanding general to expose Uriah to danger. The general did as he was told, and Uriah was killed. After David learned that Uriah was dead David sent for Bathsheba and married her. **Still trying to cover up more issues**.

Several details in the Bible show Bathsheba is innocent and shows that David had taken advantage of both Bathsheba and her husband Uriah.

1. David should have been leading his troops into battle, instead, he was home looking into Uriah and Bathsheba's courtyard.
2. Bathsheba was bathing in the courtyard of her house where she expected privacy.
3. Bathsheba was bathing at night when she expected others to be asleep.
4. David began to inquire about who Bathsheba was and after he learned that she was married to Uriah, one of his mighty men, he should have left matters alone.
5. David still sent his servant to get her so he could sleep with her, "after all, he was the king with servants and could command anyone to do whatever he wanted to be done."
6. Bathsheba was not able to turn down or refuse whatever the king wanted. She was also only a woman

who they looked at as powerless and without any rights.

7. She was seen, desired, and taken—she was violated and treated as an object, not as a person of worth and value.
8. In essence, we can look at this and see that David raped Bathsheba, she was a victim of David's lust.
9. David's fear of exposure led him to think of marrying the object of his lust.
10. Although David and Bathsheba's relationship began as an act of his lust and her being victimized by a man with power, it later became a loving and caring marriage.

ACTION STEPS:

* Always be wise enough to seek wisdom and have someone to hold you accountable for your actions, and behavior. It can keep you from a lot of pain.
* Always seek to be loyal to people that are loyal to you.
* Never seek to find your own gain over someone else's property.

THOUGHT FOR THE DAY:

Remember that sin, reveals your inner hurts and pain that's created in a decent person, and without confession, it separates you from Jesus Christ.

PRAYER:

Lord, don't let me deny my sin. Instead, teach me to honestly evaluate my weaknesses and to always take the steps needed to purify my desires and make them pure and holy unto you. In the name of Jesus, I pray. Amen.

PROVERBS 7

1. *My son, keep my words, and lay up my commandments with thee.*
2. *Keep my commandments, and live; and my law as the apple of thine eye.*
3. *Bind them upon thy fingers, write them upon the table of thine heart.*
4. *Say unto wisdom, Thou art my sister; and call understanding thy kinswoman:*
5. *That they may keep thee from the strange woman, from the stranger which flattereth with her words.*
6. *For at the window of my house I looked through my casement,*
7. *And beheld among the simple ones, I discerned among the youths, a young man void of understanding,*
8. *Passing through the street near her corner; and he went the way to her house,*
9. *In the twilight, in the evening, in the black and dark night:*
10. *And, behold, there met him a woman with the attire of an harlot, and subtil of heart.*
11. *(She is loud and stubborn; her feet abide not in her house:*
12. *Now is she without, now in the streets, and lieth in wait at every corner.)*
13. *So she caught him, and kissed him, and with an impudent face said unto him,*
14. *I have peace offerings with me; this day have I payed my vows.*
15. *Therefore came I forth to meet thee, diligently to seek thy face, and I have found thee.*
16. *I have decked my bed with coverings of tapestry, with carved works, with fine linen of Egypt.*
17. *I have perfumed my bed with myrrh, aloes, and cinnamon.*

18. *Come, let us take our fill of love until the morning: let us solace ourselves with loves.*
19. *For the goodman is not at home, he is gone a long journey:*
20. *He hath taken a bag of money with him, and will come home at the day appointed.*
21. *With her much fair speech she caused him to yield, with the flattering of her lips she forced him.*
22. *He goeth after her straightway, as an ox goeth to the slaughter, or as a fool to the correction of the stocks;*
23. *Till a dart strike through his liver; as a bird hasteth to the snare, and knoweth not that it is for his life.*
24. *Hearken unto me now therefore, O ye children, and attend to the words of my mouth.*
25. *Let not thine heart decline to her ways, go not astray in her paths.*
26. *For she hath cast down many wounded: yea, many strong men have been slain by her.*
27. *Her house is the way to hell, going down to the chambers of death.*

Chapter 7

DON'T DESPISE OTHER'S WEALTH

My son, keep my words and lay up my commandments with thee.

Proverbs 7:1

Sometimes we despise, envy, and even stop speaking with people because of the things they have obtained such as the cars they drive, the homes they live in, the clothes they wear, or the relationships you see they have with someone else. We just want their stuff for ourselves, not knowing what they had to do to obtain their lifestyle or the things around them.

Queen Athaliah how she gained the throne. Athaliah was the daughter of Ahab and Jezebel of Israel and she became the wife of Judah's King Jehoram, her parents influenced her by worshiping Baal. Athaliah's idol worship even began to influence her husband and children. During the eight years that King Jehoram ruled, his sons were so wicked that they presented all the dedicated things of the house of the Lord to their god Baal (2 Chronicles 24:7).

After King Jehoram died, his son Ahaziah succeeded him. But Ahaziah was killed during his first year as king. After his mother Athaliah learned that her son was dead, she acted quickly to destroy all the royal heirs (2 Kings 11:1). These were her grandchildren. How can she be so heartless? With the royal family wiped out, Athaliah took the throne and ruled as queen for six years. One of King Jehoram's sons survived and had been hidden during the time by God's high priest until he was seven years old. God has a way of protecting His children from the enemy. When Joash (Jehoash), had turned seven years old, the high priest organized a group.

Athaliah was executed and immediately the people went to the temple of Baal and tore it down. They broke it into pieces the altars and the images, and killed Mattan the priest of Baal before the altars... The people of the land rejoiced because they had slain Athaliah with the sword in the king's house (2 Kings 11:18-20).

The existence of a temple to Baal in Jerusalem suggests that Queen Athaliah may have been as intent as her mother Jezebel to wipe out worship of the Lord and replace it with Baal worship. Just like today, some children reject to worship and praise the true and living God just as their parents and try to impose their values. Jehoram was the son of Jehoshaphat. Jehoshaphat was a godly king who "did not turn aside from doing what was right in the eyes of the Lord" (1 Kings 22:43). Jehosphaphat made a big mistake when he made peace with Israel and married his son Jehoram to Athaliah. In doing so he welcomed a poisonous viper into his family and exposed his son to a woman dedicated to doing evil that had been influenced by her parents. So often today we don't take control of our children's lives and watch the people and things we allow into their life.

1. Ambition can be a positive thing but, selfish ambition can always bring you and everyone around you down or make you fall into the wrong kind of personal gain.
2. God can use your shortcomings as an instrument to help bring His people back to Him by your downfall, or your future generations.
3. God can and does use the worse circumstances and the worse people to accomplish His purpose.

ACTION STEPS:

* Seek to follow the heart of the only true and living God and it will keep you from heartaches.
* Never seek to have lordship over other people, making them do your will and see things your way.
* Never, seek to follow other gods. Allow the true and living God to use you for His glory.

THOUGHT FOR THE DAY:

Remember, you shouldn't try to influence others with your thinking or beliefs. Don't seek to be a self-centered individual, jumping at the chance to rule over others.

PRAYER:

Lord, don't let me try to influence others with my thoughts and teaching. And please order my steps in your Word for your glory. In the name of Jesus, I pray. Amen.

PROVERBS 8

1. *Doth not wisdom cry? and understanding put forth her voice?*
2. *She standeth in the top of high places, by the way in the places of the paths.*
3. *She crieth at the gates, at the entry of the city, at the coming in at the doors.*
4. *Unto you, O men, I call; and my voice is to the sons of man.*
5. *O ye simple, understand wisdom: and, ye fools, be ye of an understanding heart.*
6. *Hear; for I will speak of excellent things; and the opening of my lips shall be right things.*
7. *For my mouth shall speak truth; and wickedness is an abomination to my lips.*
8. *All the words of my mouth are in righteousness; there is nothing froward or perverse in them.*
9. *They are all plain to him that understandeth, and right to them that find knowledge.*
10. *Receive my instruction, and not silver; and knowledge rather than choice gold.*
11. *For wisdom is better than rubies; and all the things that may be desired are not to be compared to it.*
12. *I wisdom dwell with prudence, and find out knowledge of witty inventions.*
13. *The fear of the LORD is to hate evil: pride, and arrogancy, and the evil way, and the froward mouth, do I hate.*
14. *Counsel is mine, and sound wisdom: I am understanding; I have strength.*
15. *By me kings reign, and princes decree justice.*
16. *By me princes rule, and nobles, even all the judges of the earth.*

17. *I love them that love me; and those that seek me early shall find me.*
18. *Riches and honour are with me; yea, durable riches and righteousness.*
19. *My fruit is better than gold, yea, than fine gold; and my revenue than choice silver.*
20. *I lead in the way of righteousness, in the midst of the paths of judgment:*
21. *That I may cause those that love me to inherit substance; and I will fill their treasures.*
22. *The LORD possessed me in the beginning of his way, before his works of old.*
23. *I was set up from everlasting, from the beginning, or ever the earth was.*
24. *When there were no depths, I was brought forth; when there were no fountains abounding with water.*
25. *Before the mountains were settled, before the hills was I brought forth:*
26. *While as yet he had not made the earth, nor the fields, nor the highest part of the dust of the world.*
27. *When he prepared the heavens, I was there: when he set a compass upon the face of the depth:*
28. *When he established the clouds above: when he strengthened the fountains of the deep:*
29. *When he gave to the sea his decree, that the waters should not pass his commandment: when he appointed the foundations of the earth:*
30. *Then I was by him, as one brought up with him: and I was daily his delight, rejoicing always before him;*
31. *Rejoicing in the habitable part of his earth; and my delights were with the sons of men.*

32. *Now therefore hearken unto me, O ye children: for blessed are they that keep my ways.*
33. *Hear instruction, and be wise, and refuse it not.*
34. *Blessed is the man that heareth me, watching daily at my gates, waiting at the posts of my doors.*
35. *For whoso findeth me findeth life, and shall obtain favour of the LORD.*
36. *But he that sinneth against me wrongeth his own soul: all they that hate me love death.*

Chapter 8

MY LIPS DETEST WICKEDNESS

The fear of the LORD is to hate evil: pride, and arrogancy, and the evil way, and the froward mouth, do I hate.

Proverbs 8:13

Maya Angelou was born Marguerite Johnson; her brother, Bailey nicknamed her Maya (mine). She was born on April 4, 1928, in St. Louis, Missouri, and later moved to Stamps, Arkansas when she was three because her parents divorced and sent her to live with her grandmother and uncle. Maya and Bailey worked in Momma (grandma) Henderson's general store and her grandmother helped her develop pride and self-confidence. Later, Maya and Bailey moved back to St. Louis to live, this time with their grandfather and grandmother. One morning a friend of her mother's inappropriately touched her and she was devastated. She was raped at the age of eight by her mother's boyfriend while on a visit to St. Louis. After she testified against the man, several of her uncles beat him to death. Believing that she had caused the man's death by speaking his name, Angelou refused to speak for approximately five years. Maya thought it was her fault. She attended public schools in

Arkansas and later in California. As a teenager, Dr. Angelou's love for the arts won her a scholarship to study dance and drama at San Francisco's Labor School. At 14, she dropped out to become San Francisco's first African-American female cable car conductor. She later finished high school, giving birth to her son, *Guy*, a few weeks after graduation. As a young single mother, she supported her son by working as a waitress and cook, however, her passion for music, dance, performance, and poetry would soon take center stage. God knows it's a shame how so often things happen to us as young children and we are made to feel like it's our fault. After that, Maya's mother couldn't take care of Maya and Bailey so they moved back with Momma Henderson.

As a black girl living in the south in the 1920s and 30s, life was hard, but Maya fought against racism and poverty and no one could stop her. Maya was a strong brave girl with lots of charisma. She graduated valedictorian in 8th grade and went to high school where she won a scholarship for dancing and drama. Maya became an actress and dancer.

Maya is not only a poet, she is a historian, songwriter, playwriter, dancer, stage and screen producer, director, performer, singer, and civil rights activist! Jimmy Carter appointed her to the Commission for International Women of the year. In 1981 she has accepted a lifetime appointment at Wake Forest University in Winston-Salem. One of the most interesting events for her is when she delivered the poem "On the Pulse of the Morning" for the inauguration of President Bill Clinton.

As you can see from Maya Angelou's childhood, she detested badness and it affected her for years, to the point that she became unable to speak outwardly to anyone instead of her rebelling against other people and where she was in her life, she learned to find herself through reading books, writing poems, doing drama, and plays, etc.

ACTION STEPS:

- Be wise enough to seek to be accountable for your actions, and don't make your children feel like they're at fault for adult issues that have caused them hurt and pain. It will keep you from the heartaches of your children growing up with pains spoken or given by you.
- Always seek to forgive negative issues that have happened in your life.
- Never seek to find gain from someone else's pain. God can use your story to win them for His glory.

THOUGHT FOR THE DAY:

Remember, inner turmoil created within you can keep you separated from Jesus Christ.

PRAYER:

Lord, don't let me deny my unforgiveness. Instead, teach me to honestly evaluate my weaknesses and to always take the steps needed to guard myself. Lord, redeem and purify my desires and make them a holy gift unto you. In the name of Jesus, I pray. Amen.

PROVERBS 9

1. Wisdom hath builded her house, she hath hewn out her seven pillars:
2. She hath killed her beasts; she hath mingled her wine; she hath also furnished her table.
3. She hath sent forth her maidens: she crieth upon the highest places of the city,
4. Whoso is simple, let him turn in hither: as for him that wanteth understanding, she saith to him,
5. Come, eat of my bread, and drink of the wine which I have mingled.
6. Forsake the foolish, and live; and go in the way of understanding.
7. He that reproveth a scorner getteth to himself shame: and he that rebuketh a wicked man getteth himself a blot.
8. Reprove not a scorner, lest he hate thee: rebuke a wise man, and he will love thee.
9. Give instruction to a wise man, and he will be yet wiser: teach a just man, and he will increase in learning.
10. The fear of the LORD is the beginning of wisdom: and the knowledge of the holy is understanding.
11. For by me thy days shall be multiplied, and the years of thy life shall be increased.
12. If thou be wise, thou shalt be wise for thyself: but if thou scornest, thou alone shalt bear it.
13. A foolish woman is clamorous: she is simple, and knoweth nothing.
14. For she sitteth at the door of her house, on a seat in the high places of the city,
15. To call passengers who go right on their ways:

16. *Whoso is simple, let him turn in hither: and as for him that wanteth understanding, she saith to him,*
17. *Stolen waters are sweet, and bread eaten in secret is pleasant.*
18. *But he knoweth not that the dead are there; and that her guests are in the depths of hell.*

Chapter 9

IF YOU ARE WISE, YOUR WISDOM WILL REWARD YOU

For by me thy days shall be multiplied, and the years of thy life shall be increased.

Proverbs 9:11

Ladies, do you think about your wisdom, your dreams, and your visions as the Lord opens doors for your journey that you thought you would never take, in your lifetime? Well, let's take a look at the first lady of the civil rights movement.

Coretta Scott was born in Heiberger, Alabama, and raised on the farm of her parents, Bernice McMurry Scott and Obadiah Scott. She was exposed at an early age to the injustices of life in a segregated society. She walked five miles a day to attend the one-room Crossroad School in Marion, Alabama, while the white students rode buses to an all-white school close by. Coretta excelled in her studies, particularly music, and was valedictorian of her graduating class at Lincoln High School. She graduated in 1945 and received a scholarship at Antioch College in Yellow Springs, Ohio. As an undergraduate, she took an active interest in the civil rights movement; she joined the Antioch chapter of the NAACP and the college's Race Relations and Civil

Liberties Committees. She graduated from Antioch with a B.A. in music and education and won a scholarship to study concert singing at the New England Conservatory of Music in Boston, Massachusetts. In Boston she met a young theology student, Martin Luther King, Jr. They were married on June 18, 1953, and her life was changed forever. On April 4, 1968, Martin Luther King, Jr. was assassinated in Memphis, Tennessee. Channeling her grief, Mrs. King concentrated her energies on fulfilling her husband's work by building the Martin Luther King, Jr. Center for Nonviolent Social Change as a living memorial to her husband's life and dream. Years of planning, fundraising, and lobbying lay ahead, but Mrs. King would not be deterred, nor did she neglect direct involvement in the causes her husband had championed. In 1969, Coretta Scott King published the first volume of her autobiography, My Life with Martin Luther King, Jr. In the 1970s, Mrs. King maintained her husband's commitment to the cause of economic justice. In 1974 she formed the Full Employment Action Council, a broad coalition of over 100 religious, labor, business, civil, and women's rights organizations dedicated to a national policy of employment and equal economic opportunity. In 1995, she remained active in the causes of racial and economic justice, and also in her remaining years devoted much of her energy to AIDS education and curbing gun violence. Although she died in 2006 at the age of 78, she remains an inspirational figure around the world.

As you can look at the history and see a visual shot of Mrs. King's life, she allowed herself to be meek and humble so God can direct her path with His wisdom as He rewarded her openly for the King family name is great among nations for generations to come.

ACTION STEPS:

- Allow God to empower you with His wisdom.
- Always live so others can recognize that you are worthy of following.
- God can use your story to win other souls for His glory.

THOUGHT FOR THE DAY:

Remember, that God looks at your future through a clear lens, if you can forgive those who hurt you and caused you pain.

PRAYER:

Lord, teach me to honestly forgive those who have sinned against me and help me to always take the steps to forgive myself of past pains. In the name of Jesus, I pray. Amen.

PROVERBS 10

1. *The proverbs of Solomon. A wise son maketh a glad father: but a foolish son is the heaviness of his mother.*
2. *Treasures of wickedness profit nothing: but righteousness delivereth from death.*
3. *The LORD will not suffer the soul of the righteous to famish: but he casteth away the substance of the wicked.*
4. *He becometh poor that dealeth with a slack hand: but the hand of the diligent maketh rich.*
5. *He that gathereth in summer is a wise son: but he that sleepeth in harvest is a son that causeth shame.*
6. *Blessings are upon the head of the just: but violence covereth the mouth of the wicked.*
7. *The memory of the just is blessed: but the name of the wicked shall rot.*
8. *The wise in heart will receive commandments: but a prating fool shall fall.*
9. *He that walketh uprightly walketh surely: but he that perverteth his ways shall be known.*
10. *He that winketh with the eye causeth sorrow: but a prating fool shall fall.*
11. *The mouth of a righteous man is a well of life: but violence covereth the mouth of the wicked.*
12. *Hatred stirreth up strifes: but love covereth all sins.*
13. *In the lips of him that hath understanding wisdom is found: but a rod is for the back of him that is void of understanding.*
14. *Wise men lay up knowledge: but the mouth of the foolish is near destruction.*
15. *The rich man's wealth is his strong city: the destruction of the poor is their poverty.*

16. *The labour of the righteous tendeth to life: the fruit of the wicked to sin.*
17. *He is in the way of life that keepeth instruction: but he that refuseth reproof erreth.*
18. *He that hideth hatred with lying lips, and he that uttereth a slander, is a fool.*
19. *In the multitude of words there wanteth not sin: but he that refraineth his lips is wise.*
20. *The tongue of the just is as choice silver: the heart of the wicked is little worth.*
21. *The lips of the righteous feed many: but fools die for want of wisdom.*
22. *The blessing of the LORD, it maketh rich, and he addeth no sorrow with it.*
23. *It is as sport to a fool to do mischief: but a man of understanding hath wisdom.*
24. *The fear of the wicked, it shall come upon him: but the desire of the righteous shall be granted.*
25. *As the whirlwind passeth, so is the wicked no more: but the righteous is an everlasting foundation.*
26. *As vinegar to the teeth, and as smoke to the eyes, so is the sluggard to them that send him.*
27. *The fear of the LORD prolongeth days: but the years of the wicked shall be shortened.*
28. *The hope of the righteous shall be gladness: but the expectation of the wicked shall perish.*
29. *The way of the LORD is strength to the upright: but destruction shall be to the workers of iniquity.*
30. *The righteous shall never be removed: but the wicked shall not inhabit the earth.*
31. *The mouth of the just bringeth forth wisdom: but the froward tongue shall be cut out.*

32. *The lips of the righteous know what is acceptable: but the mouth of the wicked speaketh frowardness.*

Chapter 10

GOD'S UNSEEN PROVIDENCE

The memory of the just is blessed: but the name of the wicked shall rot.

Proverbs 10:7

More than any other book of the Bible, Esther is a tribute to the invisible providence of God. Although we never actually hear or see God within the story, there is truly confidence that He is just offstage in the background working out everything and orchestrating the drama to preserve His people from a tragic ending. Just as He still does today. It's easy to see God in the miraculous. But it's not so easy to see Him when everything around you seems to be upside down. That's where most of us live, without seeing the handwriting on the wall or hearing thunder hit us upside the head. We live without God being center stage, and sometimes we allow Him to direct us from a distance. We need to learn to be sensitive to the voice of the Holy Spirit so we can be aware and attentive to the ways He is going to work.

Esther helps us to see God's Power and His Sovereignty and she shows us how easily we can try to put God into a box or regulate Him to the outline of what we think. God refuses to be confined by our thinking and wisdom. We need to understand how mysterious God is, to make sense of the mysterious ways in which He works. Our searching for the mind of God is like surveying the ocean. You will only see what lies in front of your eyes, and miss the depth of what is ahead. In Isaiah 55:8-9, the Lord tells us:

"For My thoughts are not your thoughts, nor are your ways My ways," declares the Lord "For as the heavens are higher than the earth, so are My ways higher than your ways and My thoughts than your thoughts." God sees events even before they happen. He can see the future with clarity because He is the One who works out everything according to His will and perfect plan. Even when things appear to be out of hand, God is there working behind the scenes.

Esther was selected to be queen through a series of God-ordained events. King Ahasuerus discovered that Mordecai had once saved his life. When Queen Esther exposed wicked Haman (Esther 7:6), the king ordered Haman's execution on the very same gallows Haman had erected to hang Mordecai. Mordecai and Esther created a decree that not only saved the Jewish people. Mordecai reminded Esther that she couldn't remain completely silent, she must have been sent to the palace to relieve and deliver the Jews. Mordecai expected Esther to share these convictions and act on them.

Esther asked Mordecai to gather all the Jews and fast for three days and nights, she and her maids would also do the same thing (Esther 4:16). Esther looked to Mordecai with respect and for advice, she also respected his opinion so much that she overcame her fear and took initiative to approach the king. Esther relied on Mordecai's judgment and respected his opinion because she knew he loved her and only wanted the best for her.

Esther stepped out in faith and did as Mordecai had asked her, she said, "If I perish, I perish." Esther trusting in the hands of God, made up her mind, whatever happens, will just happen. Also being born of Jewish descent they knew the Word of God and His laws, so she just spoke what was already written. Esther, went to her husband although she knew he was a ruler and slightly a madman, people were not allowed to approach the king unless he sent for them. Anyone who did so was put to death unless the king raised his golden scepter and pointed to the person. Even Esther, who had not been called by the king was terrified at the thought of going to him. This also shows us how God's people can find favor in His Sight with kings and those that are in authority. Esther also shows us the love of Jesus Christ. In John 15:13 Jesus tells us, "Greater love has no one than this than to lay down one's life for his friends."

1. Esther showed wisdom and patience in a terrible situation while dealing with a difficult husband.
2. Esther operated within God's will in a situation and used every gift He had given her.
3. Esther was reminded that perhaps God had made her queen meet the challenge that Haman posed to wipe out all the Jewish people.
4. Just like Esther, always be willing to listen to wise counsel and advice no matter how high God allows you to rise in life.
5. Esther shows us that sometimes all of us have a skeleton or two in our closets that hangs some kind of dirt and shame over our past. These memories are not

there to haunt us, but there to help us heal from the hurts and pains.

6. Esther shows us that we can't spend the rest of our life cowering inside, crippled by guilt, we must learn to confess our sins of the past and accept God's forgiveness.

7. Esther shows us that in the struggles, disappointments, and heartaches of her family and the Jewish people, in the end, God was and still is the winner.

ACTION STEPS:

* Allow God to empower you, for victory and His glory.
* Remember God can make your regrets work so you can learn to understand His love.
* God can make your skeletons and shame from your past work out for His glory.

THOUGHT FOR THE DAY:

Don't turn your memory into a shrine, they are merely a reminder and also a means to turn your thoughts toward the good.

PRAYER:

Lord, teach me how to allow the memories of my past to be used as a pure gift until you do. In the name of Jesus, I pray. Amen.

PROVERBS 11

1. *A false balance is abomination to the LORD: but a just weight is his delight.*
2. *When pride cometh, then cometh shame: but with the lowly is wisdom.*
3. *The integrity of the upright shall guide them: but the perverseness of transgressors shall destroy them.*
4. *Riches profit not in the day of wrath: but righteousness delivereth from death.*
5. *The righteousness of the perfect shall direct his way: but the wicked shall fall by his own wickedness.*
6. *The righteousness of the upright shall deliver them: but transgressors shall be taken in their own naughtiness.*
7. *When a wicked man dieth, his expectation shall perish: and the hope of unjust men perisheth.*
8. *The righteous is delivered out of trouble, and the wicked cometh in his stead.*
9. *An hypocrite with his mouth destroyeth his neighbour: but through knowledge shall the just be delivered.*
10. *When it goeth well with the righteous, the city rejoiceth: and when the wicked perish, there is shouting.*
11. *By the blessing of the upright the city is exalted: but it is overthrown by the mouth of the wicked.*
12. *He that is void of wisdom despiseth his neighbour: but a man of understanding holdeth his peace.*
13. *A talebearer revealeth secrets: but he that is of a faithful spirit concealeth the matter.*
14. *Where no counsel is, the people fall: but in the multitude of counsellors there is safety.*
15. *He that is surety for a stranger shall smart for it: and he that hateth suretiship is sure.*

16. *A gracious woman retaineth honour: and strong men retain riches.*
17. *The merciful man doeth good to his own soul: but he that is cruel troubleth his own flesh.*
18. *The wicked worketh a deceitful work: but to him that soweth righteousness shall be a sure reward.*
19. *As righteousness tendeth to life: so he that pursueth evil pursueth it to his own death.*
20. *They that are of a froward heart are abomination to the LORD: but such as are upright in their way are his delight.*
21. *Though hand join in hand, the wicked shall not be unpunished: but the seed of the righteous shall be delivered.*
22. *As a jewel of gold in a swine's snout, so is a fair woman which is without discretion.*
23. *The desire of the righteous is only good: but the expectation of the wicked is wrath.*
24. *There is that scattereth, and yet increaseth; and there is that withholdeth more than is meet, but it tendeth to poverty.*
25. *The liberal soul shall be made fat: and he that watereth shall be watered also himself.*
26. *He that withholdeth corn, the people shall curse him: but blessing shall be upon the head of him that selleth it.*
27. *He that diligently seeketh good procureth favour: but he that seeketh mischief, it shall come unto him.*
28. *He that trusteth in his riches shall fall; but the righteous shall flourish as a branch.*
29. *He that troubleth his own house shall inherit the wind: and the fool shall be servant to the wise of heart.*
30. *The fruit of the righteous is a tree of life; and he that winneth souls is wise.*
31. *Behold, the righteous shall be recompensed in the earth: much more the wicked and the sinner.*

Chapter 11

THE PROCESS OF CLEANSING FOR CHRISTIAN LIVING

> The desire of the righteous is only good: but the expectation of the wicked is wrath.
>
> **Proverbs 11:23**

Every Christian walks in faith daily. In fact, even the worst sinners walk in faith. The central question is: what do you have faith in? Sinners have faith in things like crystal balls, psychics, tarot cards, horoscopes, lottery games, and false prophets. Many of these sinners have incredible amounts of faith. Unfortunately for them, their faith will not save them from hell, because they don't have faith in God. Do you have faith in God? Or do you simply just have faith in faith? The fact that you claim to believe is not the issue of faith. It's "what" or "who" you have faith in and believe in that will determine whether or not your faith will be rewarded. If you have little knowledge of God and His Word, you will have great faith. Is there a limit to what you can accomplish by faith? Yes. But that limit is not impossible with or by God. The limit is impossible for you.

Romans 10:17 tells you: "So then faith cometh by hearing, and hearing by the Word of God." What are you doing about increasing the strength of your faith?

However, you must remember that God is under no obligation to us. There is no way you can word your prayer so that God must get on your behalf. If God didn't say it, no amount of faith in the world will make it so. Believing doesn't make God's words true, His Word is true, therefore we should believe it.

How do you strengthen your faith? Faith is not an action word. Faith is active, not passive. Faith takes a stand, faith makes a move, and faith speaks up. To believe God and His Word, we must do what He says. If you don't do what He says you don't believe in Him. Faith is action inseparable.

Matthew 28:19-20 tells you: "Go ye therefore, and teach all nations, baptizing them in the name of the Father, and the Son, and the Holy Ghost: Teaching them to observe all things whatsoever I have commanded you: and, lo, I am with you always, even unto the end of the world. Amen." Are you walking in the mission of God?

How do you increase your measure of faith? Read Romans 12:3. He states "For by the grace given me I say to every one of you, do not think of yourself with sober judgment, in accordance with the measure of faith God has given you." So how do you increase your faith?

1. Increase your knowledge of God's Word. If you want your faith in God to increase you must increase your understanding of Him as the object of your faith.

2. If you seek to have a greater knowledge of God, you will have an increase in your faith in God. Knowledge is power.

3. The only limit of your faith is your knowledge and understanding of God, which grows every time you read your Bible, attend Sunday School, Bible Study, read a new scripture verse, think about scripture truths and Church conferences.

Wisdom, knowledge, and the power of God's Word. He tells us in 1 Corinthians 1:29-31, That no flesh should glory in his presence. But of him are ye in Christ Jesus, who of God is made unto us wisdom and righteousness, and sanctification, and redemption: that, according as it is written, He that is glories, let him glory in the Lord.

As Christians and believers in God, He has given us the ability to trust Him in His Word, but also, we must be willing to set ourselves aside to take time to learn God's Word. We must be willing to be "broken in Christ." Brokenness is a complete surrendering of your will to God's will and His ways.

Being broken for God. He tells us in 1 Peter 4:12-14 Beloved, think it not strange concerning the fiery trial which is to try you, as though some strange thing happened unto you: But rejoice, inasmuch as ye are partakers of Christ's sufferings; that, when his glory shall be revealed, ye may be glad also with exceeding joy. If ye be reproached for the name of Christ, happy are ye; for the spirit of glory and of God resteth upon you: on their part, he is evil spoken of, but on your part, he is glorified.

You must be strengthened with Christ. He tells us in Philippians 4:12-13 I know both how to be abased, and I know how to abound: everywhere and in all things, I am instructed both to be full and to be hungry, both to abound and to suffer need. I can do all things through Christ who strengthens me.

ACTION STEPS:

* Allow God to empower you for His glory.
* Remember, that you can't do anything without the strength of Jesus Christ.
* Remember, it's a good thing to be broken for God's glory.

THOUGHT FOR THE DAY:

Seek to be broken for God, so He can strengthen you for His good.

PRAYER:

Lord, teach me how to be broken for You. In the name of Jesus, I pray. Amen.

PROVERBS 12

1. Whoso loveth instruction loveth knowledge: but he that hateth reproof is brutish.
2. A good man obtaineth favour of the LORD: but a man of wicked devices will he condemn.
3. A man shall not be established by wickedness: but the root of the righteous shall not be moved.
4. A virtuous woman is a crown to her husband: but she that maketh ashamed is as rottenness in his bones.
5. The thoughts of the righteous are right: but the counsels of the wicked are deceit.
6. The words of the wicked are to lie in wait for blood: but the mouth of the upright shall deliver them.
7. The wicked are overthrown, and are not: but the house of the righteous shall stand.
8. A man shall be commended according to his wisdom: but he that is of a perverse heart shall be despised.
9. He that is despised, and hath a servant, is better than he that honoureth himself, and lacketh bread.
10. A righteous man regardeth the life of his beast: but the tender mercies of the wicked are cruel.
11. He that tilleth his land shall be satisfied with bread: but he that followeth vain persons is void of understanding.
12. The wicked desireth the net of evil men: but the root of the righteous yieldeth fruit.
13. The wicked is snared by the transgression of his lips: but the just shall come out of trouble.
14. A man shall be satisfied with good by the fruit of his mouth: and the recompence of a man's hands shall be rendered unto him.

15. *The way of a fool is right in his own eyes: but he that hearkeneth unto counsel is wise.*
16. *A fool's wrath is presently known: but a prudent man covereth shame.*
17. *He that speaketh truth sheweth forth righteousness: but a false witness deceit.*
18. *There is that speaketh like the piercings of a sword: but the tongue of the wise is health.*
19. *The lip of truth shall be established for ever: but a lying tongue is but for a moment.*
20. *Deceit is in the heart of them that imagine evil: but to the counsellors of peace is joy.*
21. *There shall no evil happen to the just: but the wicked shall be filled with mischief.*
22. *Lying lips are abomination to the LORD: but they that deal truly are his delight.*
23. *A prudent man concealeth knowledge: but the heart of fools proclaimeth foolishness.*
24. *The hand of the diligent shall bear rule: but the slothful shall be under tribute.*
25. *Heaviness in the heart of man maketh it stoop: but a good word maketh it glad.*
26. *The righteous is more excellent than his neighbour: but the way of the wicked seduceth them.*
27. *The slothful man roasteth not that which he took in hunting: but the substance of a diligent man is precious.*
28. *In the way of righteousness is life: and in the pathway thereof there is no death.*

Chapter 12

HONEY, DON'T USE YOUR TONGUE RECKLESSLY

Deceit is in the heart of them that imagine evil: but to the counsellors of peace is joy.

Proverbs 12:20

So often instead of us speaking with kindness or promoting the good of someone else, we allow the pain and hurts to show outwardly to others allowing them to attack our weaknesses and break our hearts with their evil words against us. God blessed our First Lady to help promote only the good of her husband and the peace that he will seek to bring to this county as we look at so many negative things around us, the banks not giving loans, homes foreclosed, war and so many other things going on negative in the United States, she could still hold her head up and promote peace.

First Lady Michelle Robinson Obama, was born in Chicago in 1964. But when people ask her to describe herself, she will tell you. First, and foremost, she is Malia and Sasha's mom. But before she was a mother—or a wife, lawyer, or public servant—she was Fraser and Marian Robinson's daughter. Michelle, her brother, Craig, and her parents skillfully managed a busy household filled with love, laughter, and important life lessons. Michelle studied sociology and African-American studies at Princeton University. She was a product of Chicago public schools. Michelle shares "When I was a young lawyer, there were other women and men in the firm who took me under their wing. Look for those mentors, because sometimes mentors don't find you—sometimes you seek them out. Oftentimes, they're flattered and glad to lend a hand."

After graduating from Harvard Law School in 1988, she joined the Chicago law firm Sidley & Austin, where she later met the man who would become the love of her life. After a few years, Michelle decided her true calling was in encouraging people to serve their communities and their neighbors. She served as assistant commissioner of planning and development in Chicago's City Hall before becoming the founding executive director of the Chicago chapter of Public Allies, an AmeriCorps program that prepares youth for public service.

In 1996, she joined the University of Chicago with a vision of bringing campus and community together. As associate dean of student services, she developed the university's first community service program, and under her leadership as vice president of community and external affairs for the University of Chicago Medical Center, volunteerism skyrocketed. As First Lady, Michelle Obama looks forward to continuing her work on the issues close to her heart—supporting military families, helping working women balance career and family, and encouraging national service.

Mrs. Obama was recognized for her commitment to mentoring the next generation. She adds that she has learned some valuable lessons from her male mentors, as well as the female ones. "I have always tried to put my kids first, and then ... put myself a close second, as opposed to fifth or seventh. One thing that I've learned from male role models is that they don't hesitate to invest in themselves." As we can see from the Obamas, they did not allow their words to hurt them in the race for the White House.

Michelle said when others go low, we should go high. Don't sink down to their level.

ACTION STEPS:

* Don't allow yourself to fly off at the mouth as you may block your blessings.
* God blessed you with two ears and one mouth, to listen more than you talk.
* Don't block your blessings.

THOUGHT FOR THE DAY:

Remember, don't hurt others with your words. God will fight your battle.

PRAYER:

Lord, teach me how to put my mouth in the park more, so you can receive the glory. In the name of Jesus, I pray. Amen.

PROVERBS 13

1. A wise son heareth his father's instruction: but a scorner heareth not rebuke.
2. A man shall eat good by the fruit of his mouth: but the soul of the transgressors shall eat violence.
3. He that keepeth his mouth keepeth his life: but he that openeth wide his lips shall have destruction.
4. The soul of the sluggard desireth, and hath nothing: but the soul of the diligent shall be made fat.
5. A righteous man hateth lying: but a wicked man is loathsome, and cometh to shame.
6. Righteousness keepeth him that is upright in the way: but wickedness overthroweth the sinner.
7. There is that maketh himself rich, yet hath nothing: there is that maketh himself poor, yet hath great riches.
8. The ransom of a man's life are his riches: but the poor heareth not rebuke.
9. The light of the righteous rejoiceth: but the lamp of the wicked shall be put out.
10. Only by pride cometh contention: but with the well advised is wisdom.
11. Wealth gotten by vanity shall be diminished: but he that gathereth by labour shall increase.
12. Hope deferred maketh the heart sick: but when the desire cometh, it is a tree of life.
13. Whoso despiseth the word shall be destroyed: but he that feareth the commandment shall be rewarded.
14. The law of the wise is a fountain of life, to depart from the snares of death.

15. *Good understanding giveth favour: but the way of transgressors is hard.*
16. *Every prudent man dealeth with knowledge: but a fool layeth open his folly.*
17. *A wicked messenger falleth into mischief: but a faithful ambassador is health.*
18. *Poverty and shame shall be to him that refuseth instruction: but he that regardeth reproof shall be honoured.*
19. *The desire accomplished is sweet to the soul: but it is abomination to fools to depart from evil.*
20. *He that walketh with wise men shall be wise: but a companion of fools shall be destroyed.*
21. *Evil pursueth sinners: but to the righteous good shall be repayed.*
22. *A good man leaveth an inheritance to his children's children: and the wealth of the sinner is laid up for the just.*
23. *Much food is in the tillage of the poor: but there is that is destroyed for want of judgment.*
24. *He that spareth his rod hateth his son: but he that loveth him chasteneth him betimes.*
25. *The righteous eateth to the satisfying of his soul: but the belly of the wicked shall want.*

Chapter 13

THE PREREQUISITES OF GOD'S WILL

The light of the righteous rejoiceth: but the lamp of the wicked shall be put out.

Proverbs 13:9

- Are you trying to find God's will? It's something that you have to seek on a daily basis but most people become disappointed because they don't understand what God's will is or how it works.
    1. God has a plan for everyone's life. This fact is revealed in the Bible. Read Ephesians 2:10 it tells you: For we are his workmanship, created in Christ Jesus unto good works, which God hath before ordained that we should walk in them.
    2. Not only does God have a plan for your life, but He has promised to reveal it to us. Read Proverbs 3:5-6 it tells you: Trust in the LORD with all your heart and lean not on your own understanding; in all your ways acknowledge him, and he will make your paths straight.
- God's will is clearly defined in the Bible. It is, after all, His Word. When we ask for God's will for our lives to be

revealed, first we must consult the Bible. The late A.W. Tozer wrote, "we should never seek guidance on what God has already said yes about." We should seek guidance on specific points of our lives that the Bible doesn't touch on. We have allowed methods to rule our life and not the plan God has specified.

1. God has promised specific directions for specific situations. Read Isaiah 48:17 It tells you: Thus saith the LORD, thy Redeemer, the Holy One of Israel; I am the LORD thy God which teacheth thee to profit, which leadeth thee by the way that thou shouldest go.

- There are prerequisites for you to know the will of God. Jesus outlined the first when He answered the question, "What must we do to be doing the works of God?" Jesus tells us in John 6:28-29. Then said they unto Him, "What shall we do, that we might work the works of God?" Jesus answered and said unto them, "This is the work of God, that ye believe on him whom he hath sent."

- The second prerequisite Jesus outlined is to obey the will of God in any area that we know and it should be lined up with the Word of God. The reason why God guides and instructs us in His Word is He wants our testimony to glorify Him.

- The third and most crucial prerequisite is to be willing to accept the will of God in all unspecified areas of our lives. **Romans 8:32** helps us to reflect on why we should seek God's will for our lives. He that spared not his own Son, but delivered him up for us all, how shall he not with him also freely give us all things?

- The next element of knowing God's will is through His direction in our circumstances. As you make an effort and begin to move, God will guide you. God can open and close doors in your life very easily. but as the saying goes, "You can't steer a parked car and you can't pilot a docked ship."

- God also guides us through the counsel of other Christians who is fully committed to the will of God and know Him well. This is one of the most neglected dimensions of guidance today. All of these prerequisites are very important factors. The Word of God, the conviction He gives us in prayer, circumstances, and the counsel of mature Christians are usually signs to let us know that God is leading and guiding us.

ACTION STEPS:

* Are you trying to find God's will for His glory?
* God's will is clearly defined in the Bible. It is, after all, His Word.

THOUGHT FOR THE DAY:

Remember, God has promised specific directions for specific situations. Read Isaiah 48:17 for His glory.

PRAYER:

Lord, help me to learn the promise of your glory. In the name of Jesus, I pray. Amen.

PROVERBS 14

1. *Every wise woman buildeth her house: but the foolish plucketh it down with her hands.*
2. *He that walketh in his uprightness feareth the LORD: but he that is perverse in his ways despiseth him.*
3. *In the mouth of the foolish is a rod of pride: but the lips of the wise shall preserve them.*
4. *Where no oxen are, the crib is clean: but much increase is by the strength of the ox.*
5. *A faithful witness will not lie: but a false witness will utter lies.*
6. *A scorner seeketh wisdom, and findeth it not: but knowledge is easy unto him that understandeth.*
7. *Go from the presence of a foolish man, when thou perceivest not in him the lips of knowledge.*
8. *The wisdom of the prudent is to understand his way: but the folly of fools is deceit.*
9. *Fools make a mock at sin: but among the righteous there is favour.*
10. *The heart knoweth his own bitterness; and a stranger doth not intermeddle with his joy.*
11. *The house of the wicked shall be overthrown: but the tabernacle of the upright shall flourish.*
12. *There is a way which seemeth right unto a man, but the end thereof are the ways of death.*
13. *Even in laughter the heart is sorrowful; and the end of that mirth is heaviness.*
14. *The backslider in heart shall be filled with his own ways: and a good man shall be satisfied from himself.*
15. *The simple believeth every word: but the prudent man looketh well to his going.*

16. A wise man feareth, and departeth from evil: but the fool rageth, and is confident.
17. He that is soon angry dealeth foolishly: and a man of wicked devices is hated.
18. The simple inherit folly: but the prudent are crowned with knowledge.
19. The evil bow before the good; and the wicked at the gates of the righteous.
20. The poor is hated even of his own neighbour: but the rich hath many friends.
21. He that despiseth his neighbour sinneth: but he that hath mercy on the poor, happy is he.
22. Do they not err that devise evil? but mercy and truth shall be to them that devise good.
23. In all labour there is profit: but the talk of the lips tendeth only to penury.
24. The crown of the wise is their riches: but the foolishness of fools is folly.
25. A true witness delivereth souls: but a deceitful witness speaketh lies.
26. In the fear of the LORD is strong confidence: and his children shall have a place of refuge.
27. The fear of the LORD is a fountain of life, to depart from the snares of death.
28. In the multitude of people is the king's honour: but in the want of people is the destruction of the prince.
29. He that is slow to wrath is of great understanding: but he that is hasty of spirit exalteth folly.
30. A sound heart is the life of the flesh: but envy the rottenness of the bones.
31. He that oppresseth the poor reproacheth his Maker: but he that honoureth him hath mercy on the poor.

32. *The wicked is driven away in his wickedness: but the righteous hath hope in his death.*
33. *Wisdom resteth in the heart of him that hath understanding: but that which is in the midst of fools is made known.*
34. *Righteousness exalteth a nation: but sin is a reproach to any people.*
35. *The king's favour is toward a wise servant: but his wrath is against him that causeth shame.*

Chapter 14

WALKING IN GOD'S PATH

A true witness delivereth souls: but a deceitful witness speaketh lies.

Proverbs 14:25

The gospel of Matthew teaches us that "small is the gate and narrow is the path that leads to life, and only a few find it." God's path to life seems difficult in the best and worst of times. Frequently we are instructed to do things that seem to make no sense at all. Forgive those who wrong us; love your enemy; allow people to persecute you; forsake family and friends. The list is long and difficult and seems nearly impossible for mortal man. However, this is our chosen path and we must pray daily for the strength to follow it.

1. **Will everyone who starts on the path find heaven?** Matthew 7:21-24 tell us: Not every one that says unto me, Lord, Lord, shall enter into the kingdom of heaven; but he that doeth the will of my Father which is in heaven. Many will say to me on that day, Lord, Lord, have we not prophesied in thy name? And in thy name have cast out devils? and in thy name done many wonderful works? And then will I profess unto them, I

never knew you: depart from me, ye that work iniquity. Therefore whosoever heareth these sayings of mine and doeth them, I will liken him unto a wise man which built his house upon a rock:

2. **What is necessary to stay on the path**? Matthew 22:34-40 tell us: But when the Pharisees had heard that he had put the Sadducees to silence, they were gathered together. Then one of them, which was a lawyer, asked him a question, tempting him, and saying, Master, which is the great commandment in the law? Jesus said unto him, Thou shalt love the Lord thy God with all thy heart, and with all thy soul, and with all thy mind. This is the first and great commandment. And the second is like unto it, Thou shalt love thy neighbour as thyself. On these two commandments hang all the law and the prophets.

3. **What is the importance of prayer**? Matthew 6:5-15 tell us: And when thou prayest, thou shalt not be as the hypocrites are: for they love to pray standing in the synagogues and in the corners of the streets, that they may be seen of men. Verily I say unto you, They have their reward. But thou, when thou prayest, enter into thy closet, and when thou hast shut thy door, pray to thy Father which is in secret; and thy Father which seeth in secret shall reward thee openly. But when ye pray, use not vain repetitions, as the heathen do: for they think that they shall be heard for their much speaking. Be not ye, therefore, like unto them: for your Father knoweth what things ye have need of before ye ask him. After this manner, therefore, pray ye: Our Father which art in heaven, Hallowed be thy name.

Thy kingdom come, Thy will be done in earth, as it is in heaven. Give us this day our daily bread. And forgive us our debts, as we forgive our debtors. And lead us not into temptation, but deliver us from evil: For thine is the kingdom and the power, and the glory, forever. Amen. For if ye forgive men their trespasses, your heavenly Father will also forgive you: But if ye forgive not men their trespasses, neither will your Father forgive your trespasses.

ACTION STEPS:

* Not every one that said unto me, Lord, Lord, shall enter into the kingdom of heaven.
* Lord, teach me to follow Your laws and will the Word of God.
* Lord, teach me how to talk with you in prayer.

THOUGHT FOR THE DAY:

Remember, Jesus is the only Way, Truth, and Life.

PRAYER:

Lord, teach me Your Word, Your Will, and Your Ways. In the name of Jesus, I pray. Amen.

PROVERBS 15

1. *A soft answer turneth away wrath: but grievous words stir up anger.*
2. *The tongue of the wise useth knowledge aright: but the mouth of fools poureth out foolishness.*
3. *The eyes of the LORD are in every place, beholding the evil and the good.*
4. *A wholesome tongue is a tree of life: but perverseness therein is a breach in the spirit.*
5. *A fool despiseth his father's instruction: but he that regardeth reproof is prudent.*
6. *In the house of the righteous is much treasure: but in the revenues of the wicked is trouble.*
7. *The lips of the wise disperse knowledge: but the heart of the foolish doeth not so.*
8. *The sacrifice of the wicked is an abomination to the LORD: but the prayer of the upright is his delight.*
9. *The way of the wicked is an abomination unto the LORD: but he loveth him that followeth after righteousness.*
10. *Correction is grievous unto him that forsaketh the way: and he that hateth reproof shall die.*
11. *Hell and destruction are before the LORD: how much then the hearts of the children of men?*
12. *A scorner loveth not one that reproveth him: neither will he go unto the wise.*
13. *A merry heart maketh a cheerful countenance: but by sorrow of the heart the spirit is broken.*
14. *The heart of him that hath understanding seeketh knowledge: but the mouth of fools feedeth on foolishness.*

15. *All the days of the afflicted are evil: but he that is of a merry heart hath a continual feast.*
16. *Better is little with the fear of the LORD than great treasure and trouble therewith.*
17. *Better is a dinner of herbs where love is, than a stalled ox and hatred therewith.*
18. *A wrathful man stirreth up strife: but he that is slow to anger appeaseth strife.*
19. *The way of the slothful man is as an hedge of thorns: but the way of the righteous is made plain.*
20. *A wise son maketh a glad father: but a foolish man despiseth his mother.*
21. *Folly is joy to him that is destitute of wisdom: but a man of understanding walketh uprightly.*
22. *Without counsel purposes are disappointed: but in the multitude of counsellors they are established.*
23. *A man hath joy by the answer of his mouth: and a word spoken in due season, how good is it!*
24. *The way of life is above to the wise, that he may depart from hell beneath.*
25. *The LORD will destroy the house of the proud: but he will establish the border of the widow.*
26. *The thoughts of the wicked are an abomination to the LORD: but the words of the pure are pleasant words.*
27. *He that is greedy of gain troubleth his own house; but he that hateth gifts shall live.*
28. *The heart of the righteous studieth to answer: but the mouth of the wicked poureth out evil things.*
29. *The LORD is far from the wicked: but he heareth the prayer of the righteous.*
30. *The light of the eyes rejoiceth the heart: and a good report maketh the bones fat.*

31. *The ear that heareth the reproof of life abideth among the wise.*
32. *He that refuseth instruction despiseth his own soul: but he that heareth reproof getteth understanding.*
33. *The fear of the LORD is the instruction of wisdom; and before honour is humility.*

Chapter 15

BE A TREE OF LIFE

A wholesome tongue is a tree of life: but perverseness therein is a breach in the spirit.

Proverbs 15:4

Ladies, time and time again, we feel that we can act or just talk to others in any kind of way, without thinking about the wrath that may come back our way. Their feelings, pains, and past hurt that have taken place in their life. As you can see from the Word of God, He tells us that a gentle answer can turn away wrath and harsh words can stir up anger.

If you have a sibling, they tend to be your first friend, and often they are the longest friend of your life. There is growing evidence that siblings provide a higher supportive social network in our old age when spouses have passed away, and children have gone their separate ways. Even though we grow up and go separate ways in our lives, most of the time we still never outgrow sibling rivalry. Sometimes our rivalry comes about from the parents who play favorites and leave a bitter legacy to the children who cannot or will not reconcile. Only until we come to Jesus Christ, is it possible for us to overcome sibling rivalry. Although, sometimes rivalry can also exist without parental favoritism. Let's look at sibling rivalry in the Bible.

Rachel and Leah—through Jacob's maturity in the Lord, he was not able to break the chain of playing favorites. Rachel was his favorite wife and her firstborn Joseph was his favorite son. As far as we know, Leah and Rachel were never able to overcome their sibling rivalry. For most of their adult life was a rivalry for the love of one man and it was summed up in Rachel's words "I have had a great struggle with my sister, and I have won" Genesis 30:8. In reality no one won because both sisters lived with a trail of sorrow.

Today we do not have to deal with the pain of polygamy. However, the "wife-in-law" is today's counterpart to multiple wives. If you are married to a divorced man, then you have to deal with having a wife-in-law unless you are spiritually mature in your walk with the Lord. You have to overcome the obstacles to conquer the emotions of jealousy, resentment, and bitterness of being negative in the relationship with you thinking about she had him first.

Mary and Martha—Mary and Martha had a deep relationship with God. But they even struggled with some sibling rivalry. Let's take a look at Luke 10:38-42. As Jesus and his disciples were on their way, he came to a village where a woman named Martha opened her home to him. She had a sister named Mary, who sat at the Lord's feet listening to what he said. But Martha was distracted by all the preparations that had to be made. She came to him and asked, "Lord, don't you care that my sister has left me to do the work by myself? Tell her to help me!" "Martha, Martha," the Lord answered, "You are worried and upset about many things, but only one thing is needed. Mary has chosen what is better, and it will not be taken away from her." I know sometimes you may find yourself in the place of Martha or Mary. Feeling as if you are being short-changed or your sibling is getting over on you.

ACTION STEPS:

* Lord, teach me to break the chain of playing favorites in my family.
* Lord, teach me not to ever struggle with sibling rivalry.

THOUGHT FOR THE DAY:

Remember, everyone is created in God's image and He has no BIG "I's" and little "u's" set aside for His kingdom.

PRAYER:

Father, God forgive me for creating sibling rivalry between my children, my sister, my brother, or any other family member and my friends. In the name of Jesus, I pray. Amen.

PROVERBS 16

1. The preparations of the heart in man, and the answer of the tongue, is from the LORD.
2. All the ways of a man are clean in his own eyes; but the LORD weigheth the spirits.
3. Commit thy works unto the LORD, and thy thoughts shall be established.
4. The LORD hath made all things for himself: yea, even the wicked for the day of evil.
5. Every one that is proud in heart is an abomination to the LORD: though hand join in hand, he shall not be unpunished.
6. By mercy and truth iniquity is purged: and by the fear of the LORD men depart from evil.
7. When a man's ways please the LORD, he maketh even his enemies to be at peace with him.
8. Better is a little with righteousness than great revenues without right.
9. A man's heart deviseth his way: but the LORD directeth his steps.
10. A divine sentence is in the lips of the king: his mouth transgresseth not in judgment.
11. A just weight and balance are the LORD's: all the weights of the bag are his work.
12. It is an abomination to kings to commit wickedness: for the throne is established by righteousness.
13. Righteous lips are the delight of kings; and they love him that speaketh right.
14. The wrath of a king is as messengers of death: but a wise man will pacify it.

15. *In the light of the king's countenance is life; and his favour is as a cloud of the latter rain.*
16. *How much better is it to get wisdom than gold! and to get understanding rather to be chosen than silver!*
17. *The highway of the upright is to depart from evil: he that keepeth his way preserveth his soul.*
18. *Pride goeth before destruction, and an haughty spirit before a fall.*
19. *Better it is to be of an humble spirit with the lowly, than to divide the spoil with the proud.*
20. *He that handleth a matter wisely shall find good: and whoso trusteth in the LORD, happy is he.*
21. *The wise in heart shall be called prudent: and the sweetness of the lips increaseth learning.*
22. *Understanding is a wellspring of life unto him that hath it: but the instruction of fools is folly.*
23. *The heart of the wise teacheth his mouth, and addeth learning to his lips.*
24. *Pleasant words are as an honeycomb, sweet to the soul, and health to the bones.*
25. *There is a way that seemeth right unto a man, but the end thereof are the ways of death.*
26. *He that laboureth laboureth for himself; for his mouth craveth it of him.*
27. *An ungodly man diggeth up evil: and in his lips there is as a burning fire.*
28. *A froward man soweth strife: and a whisperer separateth chief friends.*
29. *A violent man enticeth his neighbour, and leadeth him into the way that is not good.*
30. *He shutteth his eyes to devise froward things: moving his lips he bringeth evil to pass.*

31. *The hoary head is a crown of glory, if it be found in the way of righteousness.*
32. *He that is slow to anger is better than the mighty; and he that ruleth his spirit than he that taketh a city.*
33. *The lot is cast into the lap; but the whole disposing thereof is of the LORD.*

Chapter 16

DO YOU LIVE IN PEACE

When a man's ways please the LORD, he maketh even his enemies to be at peace with him.

Proverbs 16:7

Do you find yourself sometimes in conflict with others? Disagreement is part of life regardless of where you live, work, or the family in which you were raised. Sometimes you may be the reason for some of your disagreements. Everyone faces conflicts in their lives, so seeking ways to escape disagreements is pointless. You can avoid disagreements from time to time but ask yourself how you deal with them. Let's look at a few areas that cause us disagreements and conflicts.

1. Sometimes disputes arise out of simple differences of opinion because we all tend to have an opinion on everything. Sometimes our disagreement comes about just over "What's for dinner?" If it's handled incorrectly it can lead to a bitter argument.

2. Miscommunication from hearing something incorrectly that the other person said, or the way in which it was meant. Unless there is clarification, the

matter could grow into a deep sense of betrayal, simply because of a lack of communication.

3. Relationships are often torn apart because of envy, jealousy, and gossip. This commonly is a consequence of miscommunication.

4. Tensions can arise from someone's deep abiding convictions (frequently this is seen with unbelievers), in the way they treat people of faith. Despite the grace that has been given to us through Jesus Christ, believers are commonly portrayed as isolated, elitist, and "holier than thou." So often this is a critical blow to Christians who are honestly trying to reach the world for the Lord.

5. Conflicts can also result from one's baggage. Maybe the person has been physically, mentally, or sexually abused. Any of these conflicts can make a person feel worthless, unwanted, and guilty. It often lingers in the back of their mind and affects their decisions. Also, these can cause the person to show frustration and defensiveness which can devastate relationships and upset everyone that is involved.

It's important you learn to recognize these traps to understand what's going on within others, and also to bring about healing. When we respond wrong to painful consequences, it limits our potential to grow. Holding on to pride subtly convinces us that we are always right. If that's true, then there wouldn't be anything for you to learn. At that point you have locked the door to your mind, so now you don't accept any new information. When you do that, you essentially shut yourself away from the lessons that God may wish to teach you. Being unteachable shows that you have rejected His sovereign control over your life. This prevents us from discovering who we are. Without acknowledging our weaknesses, mistakes, and failures, we can never see the peace of God or His character.

ACTION STEPS:

- Make sure that you're not the reason for some of your disagreements. Read Galatians 5:14-22.
- Make sure you are walking in the fruits of His spirit, for His glory. Read Galatians 5:22-26.

THOUGHT FOR THE DAY:

Remember, conflicts can also result from others' personal baggage. you can be the peacemaker for God.

PRAYER:

Lord, teach me how to walk in Your peace by faith. In the name of Jesus, I pray. Amen.

PROVERBS 17

1. Better is a dry morsel, and quietness therewith, than an house full of sacrifices with strife.
2. A wise servant shall have rule over a son that causeth shame, and shall have part of the inheritance among the brethren.
3. The fining pot is for silver, and the furnace for gold: but the LORD trieth the hearts.
4. A wicked doer giveth heed to false lips; and a liar giveth ear to a naughty tongue.
5. Whoso mocketh the poor reproacheth his Maker: and he that is glad at calamities shall not be unpunished.
6. Children's children are the crown of old men; and the glory of children are their fathers.
7. Excellent speech becometh not a fool: much less do lying lips a prince.
8. A gift is as a precious stone in the eyes of him that hath it: whithersoever it turneth, it prospereth.
9. He that covereth a transgression seeketh love; but he that repeateth a matter separateth very friends.
10. A reproof entereth more into a wise man than an hundred stripes into a fool.
11. An evil man seeketh only rebellion: therefore a cruel messenger shall be sent against him.
12. Let a bear robbed of her whelps meet a man, rather than a fool in his folly.
13. Whoso rewardeth evil for good, evil shall not depart from his house.
14. The beginning of strife is as when one letteth out water: therefore leave off contention, before it be meddled with.

15. *He that justifieth the wicked, and he that condemneth the just, even they both are abomination to the LORD.*
16. *Wherefore is there a price in the hand of a fool to get wisdom, seeing he hath no heart to it?*
17. *A friend loveth at all times, and a brother is born for adversity.*
18. *A man void of understanding striketh hands, and becometh surety in the presence of his friend.*
19. *He loveth transgression that loveth strife: and he that exalteth his gate seeketh destruction.*
20. *He that hath a froward heart findeth no good: and he that hath a perverse tongue falleth into mischief.*
21. *He that begetteth a fool doeth it to his sorrow: and the father of a fool hath no joy.*
22. *A merry heart doeth good like a medicine: but a broken spirit drieth the bones.*
23. *A wicked man taketh a gift out of the bosom to pervert the ways of judgment.*
24. *Wisdom is before him that hath understanding; but the eyes of a fool are in the ends of the earth.*
25. *A foolish son is a grief to his father, and bitterness to her that bare him.*
26. *Also to punish the just is not good, nor to strike princes for equity.*
27. *He that hath knowledge spareth his words: and a man of understanding is of an excellent spirit.*
28. *Even a fool, when he holdeth his peace, is counted wise: and he that shutteth his lips is esteemed a man of understanding.*

Chapter 17

LOVE IN UNITY

Better is a dry morsel, and quietness therewith, than a house full of sacrifices with strife.

Proverbs 17:1

Conflicts can break up our homes, families, friendships, and communities because of incidents that have been blown out of proportion. As Christians, we are called to love one another and this love is lived out in our life with each other. The ultimate outcome of loving one another this way is a life of peace and unity. We find ourselves seeking to grow in our understanding and experience our value to God. His love for us and to understand that nothing can separate us from Him and His love. With this understanding, you know that you can't be separated from Him. So, learn to daily seek Him for His wisdom to walk in victory.

After being married for about five years, my husband was working at a job in which he had grown to be upset. He had gotten to the place where he was upset and angry with his employees almost daily because they would do something that would challenge him. He would get home every day for about three or four weeks very angry, so much so that he caused me to become upset with him. He wouldn't talk, and sometimes didn't want to eat, then I would become upset because I don't handle fussing and arguing well. After about one or two weeks of us fussing and having to ask for forgiveness before going to sleep, I had to ask the Lord how to handle this issue for Him to be glorified in the outcome. After I went to Him, instantly He showed me, that I should place on the front door, a smiley face and under it He had me write, "If our conversation doesn't give God glory at the end of each day maybe we need to speak with a smile in silence." For days he would come home and just be quiet, but I would still have him a nice dinner prepared. Years later he was sharing with me that he shared at his men's meeting about how that smiley face helped to keep peace in our home. Also, how it helped him to understand how important it is for Christians to daily grow more in love with one another instead of us stirring up anger and strife. We have grown so much more in love with one another through God developing us to seek His likeness; we share in mentoring at the juvenile detention center, Bible study, Sunday school, and feeding the homeless.

We learned in Galatians 5:13-26, "You, my brothers, were called to be free. But do not use your freedom to indulge the sinful nature; rather, serve one another in love." The entire law is summed up in a single command: "Love your neighbor as yourself." If you keep on biting and devouring each other, watch out or you will be destroyed by each other. So I say, live by the Spirit, and you will not gratify the desires of the sinful nature. For the sinful nature desires what is contrary to the Spirit, and the Spirit what is contrary to the sinful nature. They are in conflict with each other so you do not do what you want. But if you are led by the Spirit, you are not under the law. The acts of the sinful nature are obvious: sexual immorality, impurity, and debauchery; idolatry and witchcraft; hatred, discord, jealousy, fits of rage, selfish ambition, dissensions, factions, and envy; drunkenness, orgies, and the like. I warn you, as I did before, that those who live like this will not inherit the Kingdom of God. But the fruit of the Spirit is love, joy, peace, patience, kindness, goodness, faithfulness, gentleness, and self-control. Against such things, there is no law. Those who belong to Christ Jesus have crucified sinful nature with its passions and desires. Since we live by the Spirit, let us keep in step with the Spirit. Let us not become conceited, provoking, and envying each other. He showed us that everything within self has to die so the Holy Spirit of God through Jesus Christ can live.

ACTION STEPS:

* **Anger**—Hostility is a natural outgrowth of jealousy and bitterness—know how to give Him glory in your conversation.
* **Lack of peace**—Jealousy, and peace stand in opposition to each other; you can't have them both.
* **Insecurity**—you never feel as if you have enough because you have placed a higher value on what someone else has.

THOUGHT FOR THE DAY:

Our need to be right is so great that we are not willing to be a sacrifice for Jesus Christ, in order not to destroy our relationships, friendships, and even love for one another. The need to be right always produce hostility and cruelty and causes people to say things that shut off communication with each other and God. No matter if it's positive or negative, all life changes can work for your good if you handle them the right way.

Ask God to fill you with His love and spirit, so you can learn to keep harmony in your Christian walk and be able to touch others with the love of Jesus Christ.

PRAYER:

Lord, may my speech and my words always be uplifting. Forbid that I should ever hurt anyone by careless speech or an unkind word. Grant that I might speak with your grace and your love at all times for your glory. In the name of Jesus, I pray. Amen.

PROVERBS 18

1. Through desire a man, having separated himself, seeketh and intermeddleth with all wisdom.
2. A fool hath no delight in understanding, but that his heart may discover itself.
3. When the wicked cometh, then cometh also contempt, and with ignominy reproach.
4. The words of a man's mouth are as deep waters, and the wellspring of wisdom as a flowing brook.
5. It is not good to accept the person of the wicked, to overthrow the righteous in judgment.
6. A fool's lips enter into contention, and his mouth calleth for strokes.
7. A fool's mouth is his destruction, and his lips are the snare of his soul.
8. The words of a talebearer are as wounds, and they go down into the innermost parts of the belly.
9. He also that is slothful in his work is brother to him that is a great waster.
10. The name of the LORD is a strong tower: the righteous runneth into it, and is safe.
11. The rich man's wealth is his strong city, and as an high wall in his own conceit.
12. Before destruction the heart of man is haughty, and before honour is humility.
13. He that answereth a matter before he heareth it, it is folly and shame unto him.
14. The spirit of a man will sustain his infirmity; but a wounded spirit who can bear?

15. *The heart of the prudent getteth knowledge; and the ear of the wise seeketh knowledge.*
16. *A man's gift maketh room for him, and bringeth him before great men.*
17. *He that is first in his own cause seemeth just; but his neighbour cometh and searcheth him.*
18. *The lot causeth contentions to cease, and parteth between the mighty.*
19. *A brother offended is harder to be won than a strong city: and their contentions are like the bars of a castle.*
20. *A man's belly shall be satisfied with the fruit of his mouth; and with the increase of his lips shall he be filled.*
21. *Death and life are in the power of the tongue: and they that love it shall eat the fruit thereof.*
22. *Whoso findeth a wife findeth a good thing, and obtaineth favour of the LORD.*
23. *The poor useth intreaties; but the rich answereth roughly.*
24. *A man that hath friends must shew himself friendly: and there is a friend that sticketh closer than a brother.*

Chapter 18

ALLOW GOD TO FIND AND SEND YOUR HUSBAND TO YOU

Whoso findeth a wife findeth a good thing and obtaineth favour of the LORD.

Proverbs 18:22

It is difficult to overemphasize the importance of a woman's reputation. Long before Boaz met Ruth or knew her by sight, he had heard good things about her. In a small farm community, it was impossible to keep secrets. Everyone knew that Naomi had come back from Moab and that she was accompanied by her daughter-in-law, Ruth. They knew of Ruth's choice to commit herself to Naomi's people and their God, and they had formed definite opinions about her character. When Boaz first met her, he was able to say, "It has been fully reported to me, all that you have done for your mother-in-law since the death of your husband, and how you have left your father and your mother and the land of your birth, and have come to a people whom you did not know before" (Ruth 2:11).

Boaz treated her favorably. He invited her to eat with his harvesters, told her to glean with his servants, and instructed the young men not to molest her. With it being necessary for

Boaz to give these instructions, they help to remind us of how dangerous life could be for a woman alone in that era. Boaz also instructed his harvesters to be sure to leave handfuls of grain for Ruth to collect. When Naomi learned what had happened and realized that Boaz was near relative to her, she felt that God was opening a door for Ruth. She instructed Ruth to continue to work in Boaz's fields through the barley and wheat harvests. For several weeks of the harvests until it passed. Naomi took Ruth aside and explained to Ruth her concern for her future security. Naomi knew that since Boaz was a near relative, he was qualified not only to marry Ruth but also to reclaim the lands of her husband. So, Naomi told Ruth how to approach Boaz. During the harvest season workers often slept outside in the fields. Naomi told Ruth to go at night where Boaz was sleeping and lie down at his feet. This position that Ruth took was symbolic and a request that Boaz takes her under his protection as a wife. Boaz clearly understood the symbolism and promised to do as requested. Boaz took her under his protection as his wife. All the people of the town knew that Ruth was a virtuous woman (Ruth 3:11). The marriage was blessed with a son, and that son became the grandfather of King David and an ancestor of Jesus Christ.

Looking at how Boaz found Ruth, reminds me of how my husband and I met at church. One Sunday morning he saw me, and I saw him, but I thought nothing of it. The very next day, I stopped by Office Depot after I had just been laid off from my job after four years. The week prior I was coming from the unemployment office, and he came over as he saw me in Office Depot and asked if he saw me at church yesterday, and told me he was faxing off resumes. I said yes, and gave him a copy of the book the Lord had given me to self-publish and he thanked me and walked away. About a week or two later, he found my phone number within the book, called me to let me know that he read my book and had just relocated to Georgia from Miami, FL, and he was looking to meet some friends so he could have someone to talk to sometimes. I told him to feel free to call anytime. Afterward, he asked his sister-in-law about the lady he had met from the church, "me," and she told him he couldn't have met a better person in our church. The next week or so, I took a mission trip to Haiti and after I came back, he started keeping in touch with me. He invited me out to dinner, a movie, and the park. After a couple of months of walking in the park, we were walking through the park and he stopped to ask me to marry him on New Year's. This was already July and he wanted us to have a new year and a new life together. From there the rest is history. Ten years later he still tells me God truly blessed him when he met me. Ladies, the Word lets us know that man should look for us to find favor from the Lord and not you look for him. We just mess up things and take them out of the order that God has planned.

1. Ruth reminds us that it's better to establish a good reputation and to win the approval of all who know you.
2. Ruth shows us a marvelous capacity for love and loyalty to our elderly and the wisdom they can pour into us if we are willing to listen.
3. Ruth recognized and was willing to learn of the ways. Naomi lived a life worth emulating and wanted the peace, character, and loving kindness she displayed.
4. Ruth reminds us that character does count.
5. Good men are more concerned about finding a godly spouse than a sexy one.

6. Ruth and Boaz's love grew out of their commitment to values far more significant than mere good looks.

7. Both need the love of God to seek wise counsel, from our elders who love the Lord, His people, and also who are willing to speak life into you.

Being single is an important time to prepare for marriage. It can also be a time to experience a closer communion with God. As you seek God to cleanse you of the world and help you become the kind of wife or husband that would bless someone, the Lord could begin using you to bless others; then you will find yourself content in Him. Eventually, in God's plan and timing, He will bless you with a wonderful mate so that both lives can be a witness for Him. If a marriage cannot glorify the Lord, then it would be better to remain alone.

Marriage is the second major choice you make in your life, and you should never enter into it without much prayer. To rush into a marriage can be disastrous. The most important decision of your life, of course, is your decision to follow the Lord. This decision is not a one-time declaration, but a daily determination to follow Jesus above all. So many have failed the Lord because they chose a man or woman over the Lord.

ACTION STEPS:

* Seek God to send you a mate so it can be for life for His glory.
* God will pour out His heart and make you seek His Word for understanding your spouse.

* Ask God to help you keep your flesh under control until He sends your mate.

THOUGHT FOR THE DAY:

Ask God to keep you in your Christian walk so others will know and see the love of Jesus Christ before He sends your spouse.

PRAYER:

Lord, help me to walk in your ways until you send my soul mate. In the name of Jesus, I pray. Amen.

PROVERBS 19

1. *Better is the poor that walketh in his integrity, than he that is perverse in his lips, and is a fool.*
2. *Also, that the soul be without knowledge, it is not good; and he that hasteth with his feet sinneth.*
3. *The foolishness of man perverteth his way: and his heart fretteth against the LORD.*
4. *Wealth maketh many friends; but the poor is separated from his neighbour.*
5. *A false witness shall not be unpunished, and he that speaketh lies shall not escape.*
6. *Many will intreat the favour of the prince: and every man is a friend to him that giveth gifts.*
7. *All the brethren of the poor do hate him: how much more do his friends go far from him? he pursueth them with words, yet they are wanting to him.*
8. *He that getteth wisdom loveth his own soul: he that keepeth understanding shall find good.*
9. *A false witness shall not be unpunished, and he that speaketh lies shall perish.*
10. *Delight is not seemly for a fool; much less for a servant to have rule over princes.*
11. *The discretion of a man deferreth his anger; and it is his glory to pass over a transgression.*
12. *The king's wrath is as the roaring of a lion; but his favour is as dew upon the grass.*
13. *A foolish son is the calamity of his father: and the contentions of a wife are a continual dropping.*
14. *House and riches are the inheritance of fathers: and a prudent wife is from the LORD.*

15. *Slothfulness casteth into a deep sleep; and an idle soul shall suffer hunger.*
16. *He that keepeth the commandment keepeth his own soul; but he that despiseth his ways shall die.*
17. *He that hath pity upon the poor lendeth unto the LORD; and that which he hath given will he pay him again.*
18. *Chasten thy son while there is hope, and let not thy soul spare for his crying.*
19. *A man of great wrath shall suffer punishment: for if thou deliver him, yet thou must do it again.*
20. *Hear counsel, and receive instruction, that thou mayest be wise in thy latter end.*
21. *There are many devices in a man's heart; nevertheless the counsel of the LORD, that shall stand.*
22. *The desire of a man is his kindness: and a poor man is better than a liar.*
23. *The fear of the LORD tendeth to life: and he that hath it shall abide satisfied; he shall not be visited with evil.*
24. *A slothful man hideth his hand in his bosom, and will not so much as bring it to his mouth again.*
25. *Smite a scorner, and the simple will beware: and reprove one that hath understanding, and he will understand knowledge.*
26. *He that wasteth his father, and chaseth away his mother, is a son that causeth shame, and bringeth reproach.*
27. *Cease, my son, to hear the instruction that causeth to err from the words of knowledge.*
28. *An ungodly witness scorneth judgment: and the mouth of the wicked devoureth iniquity.*
29. *Judgments are prepared for scorners, and stripes for the back of fools.*

Chapter 19

GOD
RESUME OF GOD'S QUALIFICATIONS

Hear counsel, and receive instruction, that thou mayest be wise in thy latter end.

                              Proverbs 19:20

EXPERIENCE:	Before the beginning of time, and from everlasting to everlasting.
ABILITY:	All-Knowing, Always Present, and All-Powerful.
PRIOR EMPLOYMENT:	Created the universe, put the galaxies in place formed man.
	Established heaven and earth, a spoken word, and currently is holding up the world by My Power.
EDUCATION AND TRAINING:	I have All Knowledge and All Wisdom.
CHARACTER REFERENCES:	The Father, The Son, The Holy Angels, and The Holy Spirit.

Other character trails are listed in the following places:

James tells of **My Wisdom**.	(James 1:5)
Corinthians tell of **My Comfort**.	(2 Corinthians 1:3)
John tells of **My Truth**.	(John 8:32)
Peter tells that I Am **A Healer**.	(1 Peter 2:24)
Philippians tells of **My Strength**.	(Philippians 4:13)
The other John tells of **My Forgiveness**.	(1 John 1:9)
Philippians tells you that I Am **A Provider**.	(Philippians 4:19)
Ephesians tells of **My Mercy**.	(Ephesians 2:4)
Romans tells that **I Am Just**.	(Romans 3:26)
Matthew tells you **How Good I AM**.	(Matthew 19:17)

AVAILABILITY: I am willing and always ready to take over your life. I am also able to put you back together again. I will bring all of who I am into your life. I Can Start Now.

SALARY: The work in your life has already been paid for through the blood of My Son, Jesus Christ. Your only responsibility is to commit on a daily basis to trust Me and obey what Jesus Christ has done and wants to do in your life.

ACTION STEPS:

- Remember, God's experience was before the beginning of time and is from everlasting to everlasting.
- Examine your image of God and your understanding of His character and nature. Make a list of His attributes.
- Now examine your list. Are the attributes you listed based on Scripture or are they a kind of sketch based on your own experiences?
- Consciously ask God to reveal Himself to you so that you may love and revere Him as you should.
- Always remember to trust God, even if you don't ever receive a mate, maybe He wants to use you within your family, church, and community for more of His glory.

THOUGHT FOR THE DAY:

Remember, God's Reference traits are listed in all 66 Books of the Bible from Genesis to Revelations.

PRAYER:

Lord, deliver me from my view and misconceptions. Let me know and help me to remember that you are in control of my life and everything around me. In the name of Jesus, I pray. Amen.

PROVERBS 20

1. Wine is a mocker, strong drink is raging: and whosoever is deceived thereby is not wise.
2. The fear of a king is as the roaring of a lion: whoso provoketh him to anger sinneth against his own soul.
3. It is an honour for a man to cease from strife: but every fool will be meddling.
4. The sluggard will not plow by reason of the cold; therefore shall he beg in harvest, and have nothing.
5. Counsel in the heart of man is like deep water; but a man of understanding will draw it out.
6. Most men will proclaim every one his own goodness: but a faithful man who can find?
7. The just man walketh in his integrity: his children are blessed after him.
8. A king that sitteth in the throne of judgment scattereth away all evil with his eyes.
9. Who can say, I have made my heart clean, I am pure from my sin?
10. Divers weights, and divers measures, both of them are alike abomination to the LORD.
11. Even a child is known by his doings, whether his work be pure, and whether it be right.
12. The hearing ear, and the seeing eye, the LORD hath made even both of them.
13. Love not sleep, lest thou come to poverty; open thine eyes, and thou shalt be satisfied with bread.
14. It is naught, it is naught, saith the buyer: but when he is gone his way, then he boasteth.

15. *There is gold, and a multitude of rubies: but the lips of knowledge are a precious jewel.*
16. *Take his garment that is surety for a stranger: and take a pledge of him for a strange woman.*
17. *Bread of deceit is sweet to a man; but afterwards his mouth shall be filled with gravel.*
18. *Every purpose is established by counsel: and with good advice make war.*
19. *He that goeth about as a talebearer revealeth secrets: therefore meddle not with him that flattereth with his lips.*
20. *Whoso curseth his father or his mother, his lamp shall be put out in obscure darkness.*
21. *An inheritance may be gotten hastily at the beginning; but the end thereof shall not be blessed.*
22. *Say not thou, I will recompense evil; but wait on the LORD, and he shall save thee.*
23. *Divers weights are an abomination unto the LORD; and a false balance is not good.*
24. *Man's goings are of the LORD; how can a man then understand his own way?*
25. *It is a snare to the man who devoureth that which is holy, and after vows to make enquiry.*
26. *A wise king scattereth the wicked, and bringeth the wheel over them.*
27. *The spirit of man is the candle of the LORD, searching all the inward parts of the belly.*
28. *Mercy and truth preserve the king: and his throne is upholden by mercy.*
29. *The glory of young men is their strength: and the beauty of old men is the grey head.*
30. *The blueness of a wound cleanseth away evil: so do stripes the inward parts of the belly.*

Chapter 20

YOU CAN'T KNOW THE WAY WITHOUT GOD

> Man's goings are of the LORD; how can a man then understand his own way.
>
> **Proverbs 20:24**

Why are you tempted to think that you can do your own thing without following any guidelines, directions, or orders from anyone? It's your life, it's your own thing and it's your own world. Have you thought about how the day is separate from the night? The moon and stars have a time when they come out every month, and the seasons change, "Spring, Summer, Fall & Winter." The stars and the moon know just when to come out, and don't fall to the earth. In the book of Job Chapter 3, he asked God why was he born to go through all this heartache and pain. God had to remind him, just like Job, he reminds us where were you when He put the world in place and separated the stars and everything else. Where were you?

We are tempted to think how wonderful life would be if there were no pain. However, pain is as important as the nerve cells that transmit pain. If our skin is damaged and the nerve endings are not functioning, we would be in danger of destroying the rest of our body. We would not have any warning of the danger that pain provides for us. Pain plays a definite role in the body of Christ and our lives. For the sake of the church, you need to be in tune with pain, your own as well as that of others. We have to heed its warning and allow pain to do its work in us and through us. Because of pain and suffering, we are able to receive God's comfort and as a result, love others by comforting them.

Your Word is so wonderful; therefore, I seek to obey it. The unfolding of your words gives light; it gives understanding to the simple. I open my mouth and pant, longing for your commands. Turn to me and have mercy on me, as you always do to those who love your name. Direct my footsteps according to your Word; let no sin rule over me. Redeem me from the oppression of men, that I may obey your precepts. Make your face shine upon your servant and teach me your decrees.

Psalm 119:129-135 Your statutes are wonderful; therefore, I obey them. The unfolding of your words gives light; it gives understanding to the simple. I open my mouth and pant, longing for your commands. Turn to me and have mercy on me, as you always do to those who love your name. Direct my footsteps according to your word; let no sin rule over me. Redeem me from the oppression of men, that I may obey your precepts. Make your face shine upon your servant and teach me your decrees. Streams of tears flow from my eyes, for your law is not obeyed.

ACTION STEPS:

* Seek God for His wisdom, so you may know how to give Him glory in your conversation.
* God is more than willing to pour out His heart and make known His thoughts to you.
* Are you seeking to walk in the ways of God, or are you seeking to walk in the ways of your flesh?

THOUGHT FOR THE DAY:

"Fear" is best understood as "reverent obedience." Although it includes worship, it does not end there. It radiates out from our adoration and devotion to Jesus Christ with our everyday conduct that sees each moment as the Lord's time, each relationship as the Lord's opportunity, each duty as the Lord's command, and each blessing as the Lord's gift. This is a new way for you to look at life and see what it is meant to be when it's viewed from God's perspective.

Remember that in John 14, Jesus tells us that He is the way, the truth, and the life. Also, ask God to teach you to obey His Word and statutes as you read Psalm 119:129-135.

PRAYER:

Lord, deliver me from my misconceptions. Let me know You as You truly are so that I may worship and serve You as I should. In the name of Jesus, I pray. Amen.

PROVERBS 21

1. *The king's heart is in the hand of the LORD, as the rivers of water: he turneth it whithersoever he will.*
2. *Every way of a man is right in his own eyes: but the LORD pondereth the hearts.*
3. *To do justice and judgment is more acceptable to the LORD than sacrifice.*
4. *An high look, and a proud heart, and the plowing of the wicked, is sin.*
5. *The thoughts of the diligent tend only to plenteousness; but of every one that is hasty only to want.*
6. *The getting of treasures by a lying tongue is a vanity tossed to and fro of them that seek death.*
7. *The robbery of the wicked shall destroy them; because they refuse to do judgment.*
8. *The way of man is froward and strange: but as for the pure, his work is right.*
9. *It is better to dwell in a corner of the housetop, than with a brawling woman in a wide house.*
10. *The soul of the wicked desireth evil: his neighbour findeth no favour in his eyes.*
11. *When the scorner is punished, the simple is made wise: and when the wise is instructed, he receiveth knowledge.*
12. *The righteous man wisely considereth the house of the wicked: but God overthroweth the wicked for their wickedness.*
13. *Whoso stoppeth his ears at the cry of the poor, he also shall cry himself, but shall not be heard.*
14. *A gift in secret pacifieth anger: and a reward in the bosom strong wrath.*

15. It is joy to the just to do judgment: but destruction shall be to the workers of iniquity.
16. The man that wandereth out of the way of understanding shall remain in the congregation of the dead.
17. He that loveth pleasure shall be a poor man: he that loveth wine and oil shall not be rich.
18. The wicked shall be a ransom for the righteous, and the transgressor for the upright.
19. It is better to dwell in the wilderness, than with a contentious and an angry woman.
20. There is treasure to be desired and oil in the dwelling of the wise; but a foolish man spendeth it up.
21. He that followeth after righteousness and mercy findeth life, righteousness, and honour.
22. A wise man scaleth the city of the mighty, and casteth down the strength of the confidence thereof.
23. Whoso keepeth his mouth and his tongue keepeth his soul from troubles.
24. Proud and haughty scorner is his name, who dealeth in proud wrath.
25. The desire of the slothful killeth him; for his hands refuse to labour.
26. He coveteth greedily all the day long: but the righteous giveth and spareth not.
27. The sacrifice of the wicked is abomination: how much more, when he bringeth it with a wicked mind?
28. A false witness shall perish: but the man that heareth speaketh constantly.
29. A wicked man hardeneth his face: but as for the upright, he directeth his way.
30. There is no wisdom nor understanding nor counsel against the LORD.

31. *The horse is prepared against the day of battle: but safety is of the LORD.*

Chapter 21

REMEMBER HIS GRACE GUARD YOUR TONGUE

Whoso keepeth his mouth and his tongue keepeth his soul from troubles.

Proverbs 21:23

I remember when I was a young girl about eight or nine years old, I came to my father and tried to tell him something about a young girl at school and he stopped me and said it takes six months to mind your business and six months to leave other's business alone. I didn't think anything of it at that age, so I tried to tell him again. He stopped me again, this time he said it takes six months to mind your own business and six months to leave others business alone. That's a hold year of taking care of own yourself. After that sunk in, it helped me to guard my mouth and stay out of other's business. That's a year of taking care of yourself and the things related to you from month to month for your household, your bills, your food, your clothes, your family whether they're sick or healthy, it keeps down calamity in your life, and with others.

Grace and peace to you from God our Father and the Lord Jesus Christ. Praise be to the God and Father of our Lord Jesus

Christ, the Father of compassion and the God of all comfort, who comforts us in all our troubles so that we can comfort those in any trouble. For just as the sufferings of Christ flow over into our lives, so also through Christ our comfort overflows. If we are distressed, it is for your comfort and salvation; if we are comforted, it is for your comfort, which produces in your patient endurance of the same sufferings we suffer. And our hope for you is firm because we know that just as you share in our sufferings, so also you share in our comfort. We do not want you to be uninformed brothers about the hardships we suffered in the province of Asia. We were under great pressure, far beyond our ability to endure, so that we despaired even of life. Indeed, in our hearts, we felt the sentence of death. But this happened that we might not rely on ourselves but on God, who raises the dead. He has delivered us from such a deadly peril, and he will deliver us. On him, we have set our hope that he will continue to deliver us, as you help us with your prayers. Then many will give thanks on our behalf for the gracious favor granted us in answer to the prayers of many. Now, this is our boast: Our conscience testifies that we have conducted ourselves in the world, and especially in our relations with you, in the holiness and sincerity that are from God. We have done so not according to worldly wisdom but according to God's grace. **(2 Corinthians 1:2-12)**

ACTION STEPS:

- Examine your speech. What kind of climate do you create with your words? Ask God for His wisdom, so you may know how to give Him glory in your conversation.
- Do the remarks you make encourage or intimidate the people around you.

* Seek God's wisdom so you can learn to make a point of being more affirming.

THOUGHT FOR THE DAY:

"Every man must be persuaded, even if he is in rags, that he is immensely, immensely important. Everyone must respect others and make them respect themselves too. Give them great hope, they need them especially if they are young. Make them grow proud.

PRAYER:

Lord, forgive me, for I have sinned with my lips. How I wish I could take back the hurtful things I've said—careless words spoken without thinking, harsh words spoken out or hurt, spiteful words spoken in anger. O Lord, do what I cannot do. Heal the wounds I have caused and restore that which I have destroyed. In the name of Jesus, I pray. Amen.

PROVERBS 22

1. *A GOOD name is rather to be chosen than great riches, and loving favour rather than silver and gold.*
2. *The rich and poor meet together: the LORD is the maker of them all.*
3. *A prudent man foreseeth the evil, and hideth himself: but the simple pass on, and are punished.*
4. *By humility and the fear of the LORD are riches, and honour, and life.*
5. *Thorns and snares are in the way of the froward: he that doth keep his soul shall be far from them.*
6. *Train up a child in the way he should go: and when he is old, he will not depart from it.*
7. *The rich ruleth over the poor, and the borrower is servant to the lender.*
8. *He that soweth iniquity shall reap vanity: and the rod of his anger shall fail.*
9. *He that hath a bountiful eye shall be blessed; for he giveth of his bread to the poor.*
10. *Cast out the scorner, and contention shall go out; yea, strife and reproach shall cease.*
11. *He that loveth pureness of heart, for the grace of his lips the king shall be his friend.*
12. *The eyes of the LORD preserve knowledge, and he overthroweth the words of the transgressor.*
13. *The slothful man saith, There is a lion without, I shall be slain in the streets.*
14. *The mouth of strange women is a deep pit: he that is abhorred of the LORD shall fall therein.*

15. *Foolishness is bound in the heart of a child; but the rod of correction shall drive it far from him.*
16. *He that oppresseth the poor to increase his riches, and he that giveth to the rich, shall surely come to want.*
17. *Bow down thine ear, and hear the words of the wise, and apply thine heart unto my knowledge.*
18. *For it is a pleasant thing if thou keep them within thee; they shall withal be fitted in thy lips.*
19. *That thy trust may be in the LORD, I have made known to thee this day, even to thee.*
20. *Have not I written to thee excellent things in counsels and knowledge,*
21. *That I might make thee know the certainty of the words of truth; that thou mightest answer the words of truth to them that send unto thee?*
22. *Rob not the poor, because he is poor: neither oppress the afflicted in the gate:*
23. *For the LORD will plead their cause, and spoil the soul of those that spoiled them.*
24. *Make no friendship with an angry man; and with a furious man thou shalt not go:*
25. *Lest thou learn his ways, and get a snare to thy soul.*
26. *Be not thou one of them that strike hands, or of them that are sureties for debts.*
27. *If thou hast nothing to pay, why should he take away thy bed from under thee?*
28. *Remove not the ancient landmark, which thy fathers have set.*
29. *Seest thou a man diligent in his business? he shall stand before kings; he shall not stand before mean men.*

Chapter 22

ADVERSITY COMING, BUT GOD CAN PREVAIL

> The slothful man saith, There is a lion without, I shall be slain in the streets.
>
> **Proverbs 22:13**

People of God, adversity comes in many shapes forms, and fashions. These perplexing, confusing, and mystifying predicaments show up at the most inconvenient and awkward times in our lives, and the frustrating thing is that adversity does not need the invitation to enter your home.

One moment life appears to be serene, calm, peaceful, and quiet; then the next moment we find ourselves caught in the middle of a storm. For some of us, life is just one storm after another.

One of the strange things about this season is that it seems like it is lasting forever. One of the purposes God has for our lives is that we grow to maturity in our faith in Him and not in stuff or people. You know your faith is maturing by what you do and how you act during your storm and in your problem.

And when they had laid many stripes on them, they threw them into prison, commanding the jailer to keep them securely. Having received such a charge, he put them into the inner prison and fastened their feet in the stocks. But at midnight Paul and Silas were praying and singing hymns to God, and the prisoners were listening to them. Suddenly there was a great earthquake so the foundations of the prison were shaken, and immediately all the doors were opened and everyone's chains were loosed. And the keeper of the prison, waking from sleep and seeing the prison doors open, thinking the prisoners had fled, drew his sword and was about to kill himself. But Paul called with a loud voice, saying, "**Do yourself no harm, for we are all here.**" Acts 16:23-28 (NKJV)

Here in the book of Acts, we find a story about the Apostle Paul and Silas who find themselves in what seems to be a storm. Paul and Silas were called by God to take the gospel into the region of Macedonia. However, when they got there, instead of wide-open doors, like they might have expected, they ran into a season of opposition!

They are locked up and in chains because they were at the place God wanted them to be, doing the very thing God told them to do. What I love about Paul and Silas is that they still had faith in God. The text does not say they were crying and angry but that they were praying and singing praises.

This is my favorite part of the text, it says "but at midnight". I know you have heard people say that midnight is the darkest hour and it's when you're at your lowest, but what I want to point out here is that midnight is also a transition period. It is the transition from an old day to a new day. It can confuse you because when you think of transition you think of a sudden, rapid change.

Midnight transitions into just a minute because nothing changes but the time. I want you today to put all your faith in God no matter how it looks and what they say, my sister. Don't allow the code red to detour you because there is a transition about to take place in your life but you have to trust God.

Remember you are where He wants you to be. It's not time to put your faith in the things you see but put your faith in the God who holds you in His hand.

ACTION STEPS:

- Seek God for His wisdom, in your **"midnight experiences"** so you may know how to give Him the glory in your experience.
- God is more than willing to give you His peace within your midnight experiences if you open your heart to Him in a relationship, fasting, and prayer.
- Seek to stand in the peace of God during your midnight experiences or the ways to your broke through.

THOUGHT FOR THE DAY:

Ask God to fill you with His peace through His holy spirit, so you can learn to be at peace in your midnight experience as a Christian so you can touch others with your experiences and glorify Jesus Christ.

In Proverbs through Solomon, God seeks to help us understand that a fool is not someone with a mental deficiency but someone with a character deficiency such as rebellion, laziness, or anger. The fool is not stupid but is unable to tell right from wrong or good from the bad.

PRAYER:

Lord, fill me with your peace, love, and the Holy Spirit in my midnight experiences so your glory and strength may be an opportunity for me to lead others to salvation and eternal life. In the name of Jesus, I pray. Amen.

PROVERBS 23

1. When thou sittest to eat with a ruler, consider diligently what is before thee:
2. And put a knife to thy throat, if thou be a man given to appetite.
3. Be not desirous of his dainties: for they are deceitful meat.
4. Labour not to be rich: cease from thine own wisdom.
5. Wilt thou set thine eyes upon that which is not? for riches certainly make themselves wings; they fly away as an eagle toward heaven.
6. Eat thou not the bread of him that hath an evil eye, neither desire thou his dainty meats:
7. For as he thinketh in his heart, so is he: Eat and drink, saith he to thee; but his heart is not with thee.
8. The morsel which thou hast eaten shalt thou vomit up, and lose thy sweet words.
9. Speak not in the ears of a fool: for he will despise the wisdom of thy words.
10. Remove not the old landmark; and enter not into the fields of the fatherless:
11. For their redeemer is mighty; he shall plead their cause with thee.
12. Apply thine heart unto instruction, and thine ears to the words of knowledge.
13. Withhold not correction from the child: for if thou beatest him with the rod, he shall not die.
14. Thou shalt beat him with the rod, and shalt deliver his soul from hell.
15. My son, if thine heart be wise, my heart shall rejoice, even mine.

16. Yea, my reins shall rejoice, when thy lips speak right things.
17. Let not thine heart envy sinners: but be thou in the fear of the LORD all the day long.
18. For surely there is an end; and thine expectation shall not be cut off.
19. Hear thou, my son, and be wise, and guide thine heart in the way.
20. Be not among winebibbers; among riotous eaters of flesh:
21. For the drunkard and the glutton shall come to poverty: and drowsiness shall clothe a man with rags.
22. Hearken unto thy father that begat thee, and despise not thy mother when she is old.
23. Buy the truth, and sell it not; also wisdom, and instruction, and understanding.
24. The father of the righteous shall greatly rejoice: and he that begetteth a wise child shall have joy of him.
25. Thy father and thy mother shall be glad, and she that bare thee shall rejoice.
26. My son, give me thine heart, and let thine eyes observe my ways.
27. For a whore is a deep ditch; and a strange woman is a narrow pit.
28. She also lieth in wait as for a prey, and increaseth the transgressors among men.
29. Who hath woe? who hath sorrow? who hath contentions? who hath babbling? who hath wounds without cause? who hath redness of eyes?
30. They that tarry long at the wine; they that go to seek mixed wine.
31. Look not thou upon the wine when it is red, when it giveth his colour in the cup, when it moveth itself aright.
32. At the last it biteth like a serpent, and stingeth like an adder.

33. *Thine eyes shall behold strange women, and thine heart shall utter perverse things.*
34. *Yea, thou shalt be as he that lieth down in the midst of the sea, or as he that lieth upon the top of a mast.*
35. *They have stricken me, shalt thou say, and I was not sick; they have beaten me, and I felt it not: when shall I awake? I will seek it yet again.*

Chapter 23

DON'T TRY TO HELP GOD OUT

Let not thine heart envy sinners: but be thou in the fear of the LORD all the day long.

Proverbs 23:17

Perhaps if we cannot say something kind or good about another woman it would be better not to say anything at all. However, failure to say an appreciative word or an occasional compliment does not necessarily imply that there is nothing good to be said. It could be pride, envy, or preoccupation with self that accounts for the critical attitude of a woman towards another woman. Lot's wife, however, we hear nothing but criticism and not even a kind word about her. Nothing is uplifting or inspiring in the entire narrative. Every part of the narrative suggests lessons of supreme importance and we will do well to follow the suggestion made by our Lord to "remember Lot's wife." So, you don't fall into the same trap of looking back at the things behind you.

Lot and his wife could not have had a better beginning or foundation on which to build a good and happy life. They were closely related to the best man on earth. Uncle Abraham was one of the world's truly great men. People respected him for his sterling character and good influence. Lot and his family had a great example of godly influences in their lives for many years. Abraham informed them they were to leave all that was dear and familiar in the old country Ur, of the Chaldees. Together they traveled, with flocks, herds, and servants, on the divinely directed pilgrimage to Canaan. They also traveled to Egypt, and back again to Canaan, with Abraham and Sarah. It is only reasonable to suppose that Lot's wife believed in the God of Abraham. Without a doubt, she worshipped at the Altar Abraham built. If Lot and his wife would have maintained a heart for God like Abraham and Sarah, maybe they would have made it into the hall of faithfulness with the others named in Hebrews.

Lot's family realized the favor and blessing of God, but they did not realize that their spiritual lives were enlarged because of their close association with Abraham, the friend of God. Neither did it occur to them that the rich material blessing of Abraham overflowed into their pastures. So often we don't realize that still works the same way today—many people's blessings come from fellowshipping with the people of God. Worshipping at the altar with Christian parents, or being in fellowship with other believers. There is nothing better than following after a good Christian example or being an example for others to follow. Even after Lot and his wife chose to leave the safety of a godly atmosphere by moving into the dangers of the big city, the prayers and loving concern of Abraham went with them.

Lot and his wife thought they were well off materially because of their own business and intelligence. When a chance came to better themselves, they took it. Perhaps looking at the influence and prosperity they saw in Egypt. Lot's servants began to quarrel with Abraham's servants over the best places and took what they could. Abraham had learned not to set his heart on material things. He would rather part than quarrel and he generously suggested that the land be divided and that Lot choose first. This was Lot's chance to get ahead. Lot looked across the promised land with his eyes. "I have to look out for myself" and he chose the very best he saw. There's nothing wrong with choosing, as we do it every day among seemingly unimportant and important things. We choose what we eat and wear, spend, save, or give away. We all choose at times between things of great importance as well. When our children are making great choices, let us be there to counsel them, rather than letting them go their own way.

Lot's fault was not so much that he chose the best land as his motive, it was his selfishness. He neglected to think of the spiritual needs of his family, instead, he only looked at worldly gains. So often just like Lot, we choose to look at what looks best to us, and not what's best for us. The problem in this materialistic age is that we have a distorted sense of values. So often we count success by the things we own. Lot knew that Sodom was an exceedingly wicked city but he chose to move his family there anyway. When we read the opening of Sodom, it tells us it was a place of wickedness of the worst kind (Genesis 19:4-9, 2 Peter 2:6-10, and Jude verse 7). Not only did Lot and his wife move into Sodom, but they also fell in love with the sin of it. She happily walked its streets and made friends in the marketplace, took pride in its worldly culture, and enjoyed her permanent home and prosperity. Lot knew it was wrong to fellowship with such wicked people, but he did not have the moral strength or backbone to leave. James 1:8 tells us "A double-minded man is unstable in all his ways."

When Lot's wife was told of the impending doom of the city, she loved she believed it, but had a divided heart and she lingered. (A divided heart is a wretched heart, and indecision is crippling to a vital Christian life). We cannot set our hearts both on riches and on God. (You cannot serve two masters). The angel had to take her hand and urge her out of the city. However, instead of hurrying along, thankful to be spared an awful fate, she looked back longingly at the city for her heart was still there. This was disobedience to the divine command (Genesis 19:17). She became a pillar of salt. Transfixed in her backward look, she became a monumental warning to all who love the world and the things of the world. In her passion for possession, she lost everything she owned. She lost her spiritual inheritance and her immortal soul. As we look at Lot's wife we can only humbly say, "There but for the grace of God."

ACTION STEPS:

* Examine your heart and life to see if you are trusting in the Lord with all of your heart. Have you placed your life, your family, your career, and everything in God's hands?
* If you have not placed everything in God's hands, make a decision to do so right now.
* Be obedient to His guidance even if it isn't easy.

THOUGHT FOR THE DAY:

Remember that this is God's Kingdom and not yours, tell the Lord, I am afraid of your demands, but who can resist you?

Lord, help me to ask that your Kingdom may come and not mine, that your will may be done and not mine. Help me to say, "Yes."

PRAYER:

Lord, teach me to trust You with the daily events of my life, the little things, the finest details, that I may have the courage to trust You with the really important things of my life. In the name of Jesus, I pray. Amen.

PROVERBS 24

1. *Be not thou envious against evil men, neither desire to be with them.*
2. *For their heart studieth destruction, and their lips talk of mischief.*
3. *Through wisdom is an house builded; and by understanding it is established:*
4. *And by knowledge shall the chambers be filled with all precious and pleasant riches.*
5. *A wise man is strong; yea, a man of knowledge increaseth strength.*
6. *For by wise counsel thou shalt make thy war: and in multitude of counsellors there is safety.*
7. *Wisdom is too high for a fool: he openeth not his mouth in the gate.*
8. *He that deviseth to do evil shall be called a mischievous person.*
9. *The thought of foolishness is sin: and the scorner is an abomination to men.*
10. *If thou faint in the day of adversity, thy strength is small.*
11. *If thou forbear to deliver them that are drawn unto death, and those that are ready to be slain;*
12. *If thou sayest, Behold, we knew it not; doth not he that pondereth the heart consider it? and he that keepeth thy soul, doth not he know it? and shall not he render to every man according to his works?*
13. *My son, eat thou honey, because it is good; and the honeycomb, which is sweet to thy taste:*
14. *So shall the knowledge of wisdom be unto thy soul: when thou hast found it, then there shall be a reward, and thy expectation shall not be cut off.*

15. *Lay not wait, O wicked man, against the dwelling of the righteous; spoil not his resting place:*
16. *For a just man falleth seven times, and riseth up again: but the wicked shall fall into mischief.*
17. *Rejoice not when thine enemy falleth, and let not thine heart be glad when he stumbleth:*
18. *Lest the LORD see it, and it displease him, and he turn away his wrath from him.*
19. *Fret not thyself because of evil men, neither be thou envious at the wicked:*
20. *For there shall be no reward to the evil man; the candle of the wicked shall be put out.*
21. *My son, fear thou the LORD and the king: and meddle not with them that are given to change:*
22. *For their calamity shall rise suddenly; and who knoweth the ruin of them both?*
23. *These things also belong to the wise. It is not good to have respect of persons in judgment.*
24. *He that saith unto the wicked, Thou are righteous; him shall the people curse, nations shall abhor him:*
25. *But to them that rebuke him shall be delight, and a good blessing shall come upon them.*
26. *Every man shall kiss his lips that giveth a right answer.*
27. *Prepare thy work without, and make it fit for thyself in the field; and afterwards build thine house.*
28. *Be not a witness against thy neighbour without cause; and deceive not with thy lips.*
29. *Say not, I will do so to him as he hath done to me: I will render to the man according to his work.*
30. *I went by the field of the slothful, and by the vineyard of the man void of understanding;*

31. *And, lo, it was all grown over with thorns, and nettles had covered the face thereof, and the stone wall thereof was broken down.*
32. *Then I saw, and considered it well: I looked upon it, and received instruction.*
33. *Yet a little sleep, a little slumber, a little folding of the hands to sleep:*
34. *So shall thy poverty come as one that travelleth; and thy want as an armed man.*

Chapter 24

WITH GOD'S WISDOM, UNDERSTANDING WILL FOLLOW

Through wisdom is a house built; and by understanding, it is established.

Proverbs 24:3

Failure hurts! It's disappointing, embarrassing, and humiliating. I don't care how we look at it and the benefits, that come from it, it builds character, teaches us compassion, and yes it still hurts. As a woman, you hate when you fail, you are inundated with doubts about your intelligence, your abilities, and your worth. You are embarrassed and tempted to give up. Don't! Consider God's record for transforming failures, for turning life's misfits and rejects into dynamic women of worth! Throughout history, many women have had mistakes that caused a little pain and sometimes failures to their success. It's not the failure that makes or breaks you, but how you respond to it and what you learn from your failures. If you can persist despite failure, if you can maintain a positive attitude, keep looking forward, then you will succeed in life no matter how many times you may fail. " . . . . though a righteous man falls seven times, he rises again . . . ."

Vanessa Williams sang and danced in school productions and even signed her high school yearbook with a promise to **'See you on Broadway'**. After receiving a performance scholarship to Syracuse University, she left school and tried to make it in show business in New York. She began entering a beauty contest. In 1984, eventually won Miss New York and then became the first African-American Miss America. During her reign, some nude photos taken while she was younger in New York surfaced in Penthouse magazine. Although the photos were taken before her beauty contest victories, she was forced to resign her crown. Some people predicted that her future in show business was over. But after that, she landed a recording contract and released several hit albums. She began to perform in television roles and music videos and began appearing in films. She continues to alternate between recording, the stage, films, and television. Vanessa was credited with making one of the most startling and unexpected comebacks in show business history.

When Hillary Clinton lost the race as president for the White House, to our amazement after she pulled herself together when the votes didn't turn out in her favor, she greeted her dismal news and finely walked out to say instead of our party fighting against one another, let's pull together and get behind Barack Obama for Democratic nomination for president in this 2008 campaign so he can become the next president of the United States. After she walked away from the presidential campaign, she later accepted a Cabinet position as Secretary of State in the Cabinet of President Barack Obama, in 2009. Just as failure isn't final in your life, the list of men and women in the Bible who failed and yet went on to greatness is long and impressive. Esther was selected to be queen after Queen Vashti was removed. Jezebel and Ruth were both in the line of Jesus Christ.

ACTION STEPS:

* Take an inventory of your heart. Are you harboring any unclean thoughts or feelings? Things like resentment, jealousy, lust, or anger?
* Ask God "Search me, O God, and know my heart; test me and know my thoughts. See if there is anything within me, and lead me in the way of everlasting."
* Pray Psalm 51:10: "Create in me a clean heart, O God, and renew a right spirit within me."

THOUGHT FOR THE DAY:

"Almost every personal defeat begins with our failure to know ourselves, to have a clear view of our capabilities."

"The Bible characters never fell on their weak points but on their strong ones."

PRAYER:

Lord, create in me a clean heart, a pure heart, and fill me with Your love and goodness. Heal my wounded spirit and deliver me from envy and jealousy that have taken root within my soul. Set a watch over my heart, so any unclean things can't take root there. In the name of Jesus, I pray. Amen.

PROVERBS 25

1. These are also proverbs of Solomon, which the men of Hezekiah king of Judah copied out.
2. It is the glory of God to conceal a thing: but the honour of kings is to search out a matter.
3. The heaven for height, and the earth for depth, and the heart of kings is unsearchable.
4. Take away the dross from the silver, and there shall come forth a vessel for the finer.
5. Take away the wicked from before the king, and his throne shall be established in righteousness.
6. Put not forth thyself in the presence of the king, and stand not in the place of great men:
7. For better it is that it be said unto thee, Come up hither; than that thou shouldest be put lower in the presence of the prince whom thine eyes have seen.
8. Go not forth hastily to strive, lest thou know not what to do in the end thereof, when thy neighbour hath put thee to shame.
9. Debate thy cause with thy neighbour himself; and discover not a secret to another:
10. Lest he that heareth it put thee to shame, and thine infamy turn not away.
11. A word fitly spoken is like apples of gold in pictures of silver.
12. As an earring of gold, and an ornament of fine gold, so is a wise reprover upon an obedient ear.
13. As the cold of snow in the time of harvest, so is a faithful messenger to them that send him: for he refresheth the soul of his masters.
14. Whoso boasteth himself of a false gift is like clouds and wind without rain.

15. *By long forbearing is a prince persuaded, and a soft tongue breaketh the bone.*
16. *Hast thou found honey? eat so much as is sufficient for thee, lest thou be filled therewith, and vomit it.*
17. *Withdraw thy foot from thy neighbour's house; lest he be weary of thee, and so hate thee.*
18. *A man that beareth false witness against his neighbour is a maul, and a sword, and a sharp arrow.*
19. *Confidence in an unfaithful man in time of trouble is like a broken tooth, and a foot out of joint.*
20. *As he that taketh away a garment in cold weather, and as vinegar upon nitre, so is he that singeth songs to an heavy heart.*
21. *If thine enemy be hungry, give him bread to eat; and if he be thirsty, give him water to drink:*
22. *For thou shalt heap coals of fire upon his head, and the LORD shall reward thee.*
23. *The north wind driveth away rain: so doth an angry countenance a backbiting tongue.*
24. *It is better to dwell in the corner of the housetop, than with a brawling woman and in a wide house.*
25. *As cold waters to a thirsty soul, so is good news from a far country.*
26. *A righteous man falling down before the wicked is as a troubled fountain, and a corrupt spring.*
27. *It is not good to eat much honey: so for men to search their own glory is not glory.*
28. *He that hath no rule over his own spirit is like a city that is broken down, and without walls.*

Chapter 25

DON'T SEEK GOD'S BLESSING ON YOUR PLANS

Every word of God is pure: he is a shield unto them that put their trust in him.

Proverbs 30:5

A tremendous responsibility lies with women, whether they are married or single, for it is their hand that rocks the cradle and rules the world. The mother has a big role in influencing and molding the character of the child, this can sometimes determine the destiny of the child and outweigh any other influences. It's very alarming the increasing number of broken homes due to divorce and single-family parenting in America. Anymore the rooting of the nation is established in the integration of families. It is believed that juvenile delinquency is caused by the disruption of families in our social structure. If the family is the basis of our society, when the structure falls, homes disintegrate. Studies have revealed that almost as many juvenile delinquents come from homes where there are emotional conflicts, tensions, and attitudes that trigger family disorganization. These families and homes are broken and morally shattered just as much as divorced ones.

Often, irresponsible or criminal-minded people will blame social situations and personal relationships for their continual quarreling with their parents. As we look at the life of Hagar, we will see there were serious family problems, and it will show us once again that all Scripture is given for reproof, correction, and instruction to live a blessed life without turmoil.

Hagar occupied an important place in the intimate family circle of Abraham and Sarah. In her close association with Sarah, she learned about her God. She learned that the Egyptian gods were idols and that there was only one true God. Hagar soon heard about the son whom God had promised to give, sometimes Abraham and Sarah would talk about it with assurance and other times with doubt, but always longing for the day. The son of promise was to inherit all the promises given to Abraham, and in him, all the families of the earth would be blessed. What a privilege it was for Hagar to be shared this dream. As the years passed, she looked forward to the day when Sarah would be completely blessed and Abraham would be the proud father of the promised heir.

For Sarah these ten years that Hagar was with her, she was desperate with waiting and longing. Like any normal woman, Sarah was ashamed of her sterility. She was getting along in years and her beauty was fading. So, Sarah thought about her maid, Hagar, having the promised son for Abraham, so she talked it over with her husband about having a secondary wife, because that was accepted in those days, and her motive was good. It took humility to allow another woman the honor of being the mother of the son she had claimed by faith. With pity for Sarah, Abraham agreed to the plan of having a child with Hagar. No matter how noble this appeared to Abraham and Sarah, they both sinned. This was a clear violation of God's law

(Genesis 2:24). Sarah also put a dangerous temptation in Abraham's way and it was wrong for them to use Hagar in this way, also without her consent. This showed a lack of faith for Abraham and Sarah, together they arranged for themselves the child that God had promised to give by faith. Often, today we still make plans and take on things without asking God for guidance. We go to thank God for what we have procured for ourselves. These choices lead to headaches, heartaches, and pains that we've created for ourselves, instead of waiting on God. After they agreed to their way of helping God out instead of waiting, Sarah called Hagar and gave her to Abraham and he took her to be his wife. This is where the marital triangle began to shatter the family's peace and God's morals for them.

Abraham and Hagar's son is born, following the command of the angel, Abraham calls him Ishmael. Though the unhappy circumstances surrounding the birth of Ishmael had tremendously disturbed the domestic scene, Abraham now had his son and was very pleased! He loved him and tried to teach him the fear of the Lord. This father-and-son bond grew between them, as did their close relationship. After thirteen years together, the Lord came to talk with Abraham again. Abraham was baffled by the news that Ishmael was not the promised seed, and he prayed to the Lord, "O that Ishmael might live before thee!" But God answered, "Sarah thy wife shall bear thee a son indeed; and thou shall call his name Isaac: and I will establish my covenant with him." (Genesis 17:19).

Hagar and Ishmael are now outcasts! Abraham now has his promised and long-awaited son born to Sarah in her old age, and now Sarah has great rejoicing in the household with her son Isaac born. Ishmael couldn't understand the change of him any longer being favored and getting the attention of Abraham. It was little Isaac who was pampered and the center of attention. Ishmael was just like any normal thirteen years old boy who couldn't understand the change of him not being favored and Isaac getting everyone's attention. Ishmael taunted and teased Isaac, which irritated Sarah, then she told Abraham to cast out the bondwoman and her son. Hagar and Ishmael are cast out into the hot sands of the desert; there is not a tree in sight, no water to relieve the agonizing thirst of those in the scorching desert sun. Hagar feels lost and helpless from the agony of thirst, and her precious son lies dying of thirst. There is the quietness of death until, suddenly, Hagar is crying and sobs when she hears a voice. It is an angel who says, "What discomfort thee, Hagar?" Sarah's sin was still finding her, with disintegration in the home and trouble with the children. How different the home would have been if Ishmael had been disciplined and taught to have respect and consideration for others in his family.

ACTION STEPS:

* Don't seek to help God with His plan for direction for your life.
* If you are in a family with stepchildren, teach them to respect one another.
* Which way are you seeking, to walk in God or the ways of your flesh?

THOUGHT FOR THE DAY:

Ask God to give you patience, so you can wait on His timing in faith and teach your children to respect others, so as they grow up they will not sow seeds of disrespect and disobedience to adults.

PRAYER:

Lord, teach me how to wait patiently and walk in faith. In the name of Jesus, I pray. Amen.

PROVERBS 26

1. As snow in summer, and as rain in harvest, so honour is not seemly for a fool.
2. As the bird by wandering, as the swallow by flying, so the curse causeless shall not come.
3. A whip for the horse, a bridle for the ass, and a rod for the fool's back.
4. Answer not a fool according to his folly, lest thou also be like unto him.
5. Answer a fool according to his folly, lest he be wise in his own conceit.
6. He that sendeth a message by the hand of a fool cutteth off the feet, and drinketh damage.
7. The legs of the lame are not equal: so is a parable in the mouth of fools.
8. As he that bindeth a stone in a sling, so is he that giveth honour to a fool.
9. As a thorn goeth up into the hand of a drunkard, so is a parable in the mouths of fools.
10. The great God that formed all things both rewardeth the fool, and rewardeth transgressors.
11. As a dog returneth to his vomit, so a fool returneth to his folly.
12. Seest thou a man wise in his own conceit? there is more hope of a fool than of him.
13. The slothful man saith, There is a lion in the way; a lion is in the streets.
14. As the door turneth upon his hinges, so doth the slothful upon his bed.
15. The slothful hideth his hand in his bosom; it grieveth him to bring it again to his mouth.

16. *The sluggard is wiser in his own conceit than seven men that can render a reason.*
17. *He that passeth by, and meddleth with strife belonging not to him, is like one that taketh a dog by the ears.*
18. *As a mad man who casteth firebrands, arrows, and death,*
19. *So is the man that deceiveth his neighbour, and saith, Am not I in sport?*
20. *Where no wood is, there the fire goeth out: so where there is no talebearer, the strife ceaseth.*
21. *As coals are to burning coals, and wood to fire; so is a contentious man to kindle strife.*
22. *The words of a talebearer are as wounds, and they go down into the innermost parts of the belly.*
23. *Burning lips and a wicked heart are like a potsherd covered with silver dross.*
24. *He that hateth dissembleth with his lips, and layeth up deceit within him;*
25. *When he speaketh fair, believe him not: for there are seven abominations in his heart.*
26. *Whose hatred is covered by deceit, his wickedness shall be shewed before the whole congregation.*
27. *Whoso diggeth a pit shall fall therein: and he that rolleth a stone, it will return upon him.*
28. *A lying tongue hateth those that are afflicted by it; and a flattering mouth worketh ruin.*

Chapter 26

ACCEPTING GOD'S RULES FOR LIVING

> The words of a talebearer are as wounds, and they go down into the innermost parts of the belly.
>
> **Proverbs 26:22**

Holy Convocation—The title "Deuteronomy" originated with the Septuagint, the Greek translation of the Old Testament produced by Jewish scholars prior to the time of Christ.

"Deuteronomy" literally means "second law." It was not a second law but a repetition of the law already given by Moses on Mount Sinai. Knowing that his own time was short (Deuteronomy 3:23-28), Moses gathered the people of Israel on the plains of Moab and reiterated God's law to them. Not only were they also enjoined to "learn them, and keep them, and do them," but far too many people know what God's Word says but are unwilling to obey. As James said, "But be ye doers of the word and not hearers only" (James 1:22).

Holy Covenant—Horeb is another name for Sinai. This was the place where God made a covenant with Israel. While the Old Testament mentions several covenants God made with men, as well as covenants between men, the covenant made at Sinai was the primary one between God and Israel. Jeremiah envisioned a "new covenant" (Jeremiah 31:31), which was fulfilled in Christ (Galatians 3:24; Heb 8:7-13). The covenant at Horeb was made not just with the Israelites present at that time (most had since died) but also with those standing before Moses right now (Deuteronomy 5:3). This covenant would also be in force for future generations. Depending on their obedience or disobedience, blessings or curses would come upon the nation of Israel.

Holy God—The fact that God had rescued Israel from bondage was reason enough for them to serve God. Clearly, Israel did not choose to serve God first; rather God had sovereignly selected them to be His chosen people. Since there is but one true God, it stands to reason that Yahweh would declare, "Thou shalt have none other gods before me" (Deuteronomy 5:7). While such a command may seem basic to us, monotheism was virtually unheard of in the ancient world. The worship of pagan gods was a strong temptation for Israel throughout much of her history. Missionaries testify that polytheism is alive and well in today's world. Even in nations with a strong Christian heritage, pagan religions continue to make inroads. Among sophisticated people, the worship of other gods is usually more subtle. Such things as possessions, popularity, power, and position can become other gods. Anything that stands between us and serving God is a false god and a breach of His commandments.

Hollow gods—Closely related to the prohibition against worshiping other gods is the commandment not to make any graven images to bow down before. Since idolatry became a besetting sin for Israel, the Old Testament is replete with examples of their failure in this regard. We also see many admonitions emphasizing the futility of idolatry (Isaiah 44:9-

20). Since He is a "jealous God" (Deuteronomy 5:9), Yahweh demanded total allegiance from His people. To fashion anything as an object of worship is to diminish the majesty of the true God. Nothing in the universe is worthy to depict God's greatness and glory. For men to think that anything they could fashion with their hands could represent the eternal God is the height of arrogance.

Holy name—Since God Himself is holy, it makes sense that His name is to be kept holy, or reverenced. Therefore, God's name should never be used in a light, or casual manner. The command not to take God's name in vain does not, however, forbid using His name; it simply warns us against misusing it. The frequency with which God's name is used in common speech has increased in our world. Nevertheless, the Lord will hold accountable everyone who takes His name in vain. "The third commandment is a directive against using God's name in a manipulative way, His name is not to be used in magic or to curse someone. Today a Christian who uses God's name flippantly or falsely attributes a wrong act to God, has broken this commandment.

When Moses addressed the people as "Israel," it was a clear indication that what he was about to say was intended not for the nations around them but for the Lord, God's law was given for God's people. There were three reactions Moses wanted to see in the people once he gave the law to Israel. First, they had to learn what he was telling them. They needed to know the statutes and judgments of the Lord. A people cannot obey that which they do not know. This is why parents and the church together need to teach the Word of God to all who listen. Second, they need to keep what they heard. Safeguard, protect, and cherish that which they were given. See the value of the teaching of God's Word and hang on to it. Third, they were to obey it. To know and have it would do nothing for them if they did not incorporate it into their day-to-day living. God's Word gives guidance for life. So, we should consult and follow it as the events of each day unfold. We may read and study the Word, but if we do not put it into practice, we will be like those who do not have it at all.

ACTION STEPS:

* Seek God to identify if the circle of associates who you hang around is demonstrating godly wisdom and holiness.

THOUGHT FOR THE DAY:

"Wisdom is your perspective on life, your sense of balance, your understanding of how the various parts and principles apply and relate to each other. It embraces judgment, discernment, and comprehension. It is a gestalt or oneness, an integrated wholeness."

Stephen R. Covey

PRAYER:

Lord, give me the desire to seek Your Holiness and wisdom and the discipline to do those things that will prepare me to receive it. In the name of Jesus, I pray. Amen.

PROVERBS 27

1. Boast not thyself of to morrow; for thou knowest not what a day may bring forth.
2. Let another man praise thee, and not thine own mouth; a stranger, and not thine own lips.
3. A stone is heavy, and the sand weighty; but a fool's wrath is heavier than them both.
4. Wrath is cruel, and anger is outrageous; but who is able to stand before envy?
5. Open rebuke is better than secret love.
6. Faithful are the wounds of a friend; but the kisses of an enemy are deceitful.
7. The full soul loatheth an honeycomb; but to the hungry soul every bitter thing is sweet.
8. As a bird that wandereth from her nest, so is a man that wandereth from his place.
9. Ointment and perfume rejoice the heart: so doth the sweetness of a man's friend by hearty counsel.
10. Thine own friend, and thy father's friend, forsake not; neither go into thy brother's house in the day of thy calamity: for better is a neighbour that is near than a brother far off.
11. My son, be wise, and make my heart glad, that I may answer him that reproacheth me.
12. A prudent man foreseeth the evil, and hideth himself; but the simple pass on, and are punished.
13. Take his garment that is surety for a stranger, and take a pledge of him for a strange woman.
14. He that blesseth his friend with a loud voice, rising early in the morning, it shall be counted a curse to him.

15. *A continual dropping in a very rainy day and a contentious woman are alike.*
16. *Whosoever hideth her hideth the wind, and the ointment of his right hand, which bewrayeth itself.*
17. *Iron sharpeneth iron; so a man sharpeneth the countenance of his friend.*
18. *Whoso keepeth the fig tree shall eat the fruit thereof: so he that waiteth on his master shall be honoured.*
19. *As in water face answereth to face, so the heart of man to man.*
20. *Hell and destruction are never full; so the eyes of man are never satisfied.*
21. *As the fining pot for silver, and the furnace for gold; so is a man to his praise.*
22. *Though thou shouldest bray a fool in a mortar among wheat with a pestle, yet will not his foolishness depart from him.*
23. *Be thou diligent to know the state of thy flocks, and look well to thy herds.*
24. *For riches are not for ever: and doth the crown endure to every generation?*
25. *The hay appeareth, and the tender grass sheweth itself, and herbs of the mountains are gathered.*
26. *The lambs are for thy clothing, and the goats are the price of the field.*
27. *And thou shalt have goats' milk enough for thy food, for the food of thy household, and for the maintenance for thy maidens.*

Chapter 27

LORD, TEACH ME HOW TO BE A LIFE GIVER

A continual dropping on a very rainy day and a contentious woman are alike.

Proverbs 27:15

God created Adam and placed him in the garden only to determine that "it is not good for the man to be alone" (Genesis 2:15), He did not create the animals to be man's loyal companion. God created women to fill the void in his life. In Hebrew, she was called an Ezer. The word "ezer" means "helper." Helper not only means a domestic term of helper because Adam didn't need someone to cook for him, clean up after him, or care for him. The problem was that Adam's life was void of companionship to work with him, rule the earth with him, love him, procreate with him, and after the fall, struggle with him. God decided Adam needed someone with words. "Then God said, let us make man in our own image ... So God created man in his own image, in the image of God he created him; male and female He created them (Genesis 1:26-27). All through the Bible the word "man" refers to "mankind." The word "man" means the offspring of a "hu-man." This is pointed out because as you can see within many of the verses, the word will use "man" or "she" but they pertain to humankind.

Words Can Break a Man

Samson was chosen during a time when the judges ruled Israel. From birth, he was destined to liberate Israel from the Philistines. While Samson was strong in body, he was very weak in character. One of his character flaws was his weakness for women. Samson, regardless of his parent's warnings, decided he had to have a Philistine woman, so he married her, and she slowly but surely used her words to lead him astray. Whatever he told his wife in private, she told her Philistine friends so they could use it against him. After Samson separated from his first wife and went back home to his people and family, he married another woman named Delilah. Yet again, the Philistines saw a pathway to discovering the secret of Samson's supernatural strength. The Philistine officials offered Delilah 1100 shekels of silver to uncover the secret of his supernatural strength so they can overpower him and subdue him (Judges 16:5). Samson caved into his wife, nagging, and telling him that he doesn't love her because he wouldn't tell her the secret of his great strength. Samson couldn't take Delilah's nagging any longer day after day he was tired to death (Judges 16:15-16). He told her because he was a Nazirite set apart from God since birth. "No razor has ever been used on my head, if my head were shaved, my strength would leave me, and I would become as weak as any other man." (Judges 16:17).

After Samson divulged the secret of his strength, Delilah had him to put his head in her lap, put him to sleep, and then called for the enemies to come shave his head. Samson's strength was going out of him with each swipe of the blade. He was bound, blinded, and spent the rest of his days in bondage, because of the power of a woman's ill-spoken words. This is not the only example of a woman in the Bible who used her words to bring harm to her husband.

Michal spoke against her husband, King David, for dancing recklessly before the Lord. Her words brought a curse on her own life. She could not bear any more children.

Sarai used her words to convince her husband, Abram, to sleep with her servant girl rather than wait on God's promise to provide an heir through her. Her words resulted in the birth of Ishmael and the resulting conflict between the Arab and Jewish nations that still rages to this day.

Eve used her words to convince her husband, Adam, to eat the forbidden fruit. Her words resulted in sin, condemnation, and spiritual death for every man and woman born under the curse.

Just as sin was ushered into the world through the words of Eve, salvation and hope were ushered into the world by the words of Mary. When the angel Gabriel came to the young teenage virgin and announced that she would conceive a child by the immaculate conception of the Holy Spirit, she replied, "Behold, the bond slave of the Lord; may it be done to me according to your word" (Luke 1:38). She embraced God's will for her life and used her words to glorify Him in one of the most beautiful songs of praise recorded in (Luke 1:46-55).

Words Can Hold Back a Man

A nagging wife is annoying just like a constant dripping. "Put a guard over your mouth." Have you ever made a pot of coffee and forgotten to put in a filter for the coffee grains? It smells so good, just like you can't wait to drink a cup. You pour that coffee into a cup, then taste how nasty all those grains taste in your mouth. That's just like your coarse and bitter speech, all you can do is pour the whole pot out and start over. You need to ask God to install a filter between your brain and your mouth. To help you choose your words carefully and speak in a smooth and mellow tone with everyone, not picking and choosing who you will speak to smoothly.

Words Can Make a Man

Billy Graham is one of the greatest evangelists of our time. His relationship and mission with Jesus Christ have reached more than two billion people around the world. It began in a one-room office in Minneapolis, Minnesota, in 1950. He grew to become the Billy Graham Evangelistic Association and has taken the gospel to the farthest corners of the world. Even though Mr. Graham has been celebrated by presidents, the press, and other people for his preaching and passion for the gospel, he would always be quick to say that it is his wife, Ruth, who deserves the praise. "Ruth and I were called by God as a team, she urged me to go, saying 'God has given you the gift of an evangelist. I'll back you. I'll raise the children and you travel and preach.' I would come home and she had everything organized and so calmed down that they all seemed to love me. But this was because Ruth taught them to." It was Billy Graham who faced the multitudes as they gazed upon his fiery sermons that drew thousands to Christ, but it was Ruth, who gave him the courage and strength to do what God had called him to do. His children were good about him being gone so much because they knew why he was gone. Because of the power of one woman's words, it encouraged the passion for the gospel and the urgency of the message that their father preached.

The dictionary defines "encouragement" as "the act of inspiring others with renewed courage, renewed spirit, or renewed hope." Yes, love believes in all things. It sticks up the seemingly impossible dreams, cheering as his dreams come forward and applauding when they come true. Delilah used her words to break her man, Ruth used her words to make her man. Do you think it is best to follow in the character of Ruth or Delilah?

Words Can Motivate a Man

Things Never to Say to Your Husband

- I told you
- You're always in a bad mood
- All you do is complain
- I can't do anything to please you
- You made your bed; now lie in it
- You never listen to me
- I don't know why I put up with you
- I can talk until I'm blue in the face and it doesn't do any good
- If you don't like it, you know where the door is
- What's your problem?
- You think you are always right
- You don't own me

- You never help me around the house
- You are such a baby
- You think it's all about you
- How many times do I have to tell you
- What do you want now

Things Your Husband Loves to Hear

- I've been thinking about you all-day
- I've been praying for you
- The best part of my day is when you come home
- You are a gift to me from God
- I thank God for you
- You are so wonderful
- I don't feel complete without you
- You are my best friend
- I love spending time with you
- Thanks for taking such good care of me
- I will always love you
- You are my knight in shining armor
- I can always count on you
- You are such an inspiration to me
- You are a wonderful father
- You could give classes to other men on how to be a great husband
- I believe in you

ACTION STEPS:

* Ask God to give you a compassionate heart for your mate, and all other relationships.
* Ask God what He would have you do, to meet the needs of others with compassion.

THOUGHT FOR THE DAY:

Ask God to fill you with His wisdom, and love by His holy spirit, so you can learn to keep harmony in your Christian walk. Also, to touch others with the love of Jesus Christ.

PRAYER:

Lord, forgive me of the times that I am insensitive and not showing compassion to others, letting your light shine in me for your glory. In the name of Jesus, I pray. Amen.

PROVERBS 28

1. *The wicked flee when no man pursueth: but the righteous are bold as a lion.*
2. *For the transgression of a land many are the princes thereof: but by a man of understanding and knowledge the state thereof shall be prolonged.*
3. *A poor man that oppresseth the poor is like a sweeping rain which leaveth no food.*
4. *They that forsake the law praise the wicked: but such as keep the law contend with them.*
5. *Evil men understand not judgment: but they that seek the LORD understand all things.*
6. *Better is the poor that walketh in his uprightness, than he that is perverse in his ways, though he be rich.*
7. *Whoso keepeth the law is a wise son: but he that is a companion of riotous men shameth his father.*
8. *He that by usury and unjust gain increaseth his substance, he shall gather it for him that will pity the poor.*
9. *He that turneth away his ear from hearing the law, even his prayer shall be abomination.*
10. *Whoso causeth the righteous to go astray in an evil way, he shall fall himself into his own pit: but the upright shall have good things in possession.*
11. *The rich man is wise in his own conceit; but the poor that hath understanding searcheth him out.*
12. *When righteous men do rejoice, there is great glory: but when the wicked rise, a man is hidden.*
13. *He that covereth his sins shall not prosper: but whoso confesseth and forsaketh them shall have mercy.*

14. *Happy is the man that feareth alway: but he that hardeneth his heart shall fall into mischief.*
15. *As a roaring lion, and a ranging bear; so is a wicked ruler over the poor people.*
16. *The prince that wanteth understanding is also a great oppressor: but he that hateth covetousness shall prolong his days.*
17. *A man that doeth violence to the blood of any person shall flee to the pit; let no man stay him.*
18. *Whoso walketh uprightly shall be saved: but he that is perverse in his ways shall fall at once.*
19. *He that tilleth his land shall have plenty of bread: but he that followeth after vain persons shall have poverty enough.*
20. *A faithful man shall abound with blessings: but he that maketh haste to be rich shall not be innocent.*
21. *To have respect of persons is not good: for for a piece of bread that man will transgress.*
22. *He that hasteth to be rich hath an evil eye, and considereth not that poverty shall come upon him.*
23. *He that rebuketh a man afterwards shall find more favour than he that flattereth with the tongue.*
24. *Whoso robbeth his father or his mother, and saith, It is no transgression; the same is the companion of a destroyer.*
25. *He that is of a proud heart stirreth up strife: but he that putteth his trust in the LORD shall be made fat.*
26. *He that trusteth in his own heart is a fool: but whoso walketh wisely, he shall be delivered.*
27. *He that giveth unto the poor shall not lack: but he that hideth his eyes shall have many a curse.*
28. *When the wicked rise, men hide themselves: but when they perish, the righteous increase.*

Chapter 28

LORD I JUST WANT TO STAY IN YOUR PRESENCE

Happy is the man that feareth alway: but he that hardeneth his heart shall fall into mischief.

Proverbs 28:14

Among the women, Mary Magdalene's life shows us a vivid example of what Jesus Christ can do for a human soul. Her story begins with the darkest of all human misery and ends with the most glorious day in the history of the world.

Mary's home was in Magdala, a small town on the western shore of the Sea of Galilee. An ugly stigma had been attached to her name from the earliest times, and she became known as the reclaimed of the fallen woman redeemed to sainthood. Because at that time, the identification of Mary was with the sinful woman who anointed the feet of Jesus in Simon's house (Luke 7:36-50). The Roman Catholic church perpetuated this infamy by building a house for fallen women. But Luke 8:2 tells us that Mary followed Jesus on His preaching tours to minister to His needs after she had been healed of infirmities and evil spirits. She was released from the torture of seven devils (Mark 16:9). It seems that all the forces of hell were let loose to raise havoc as the Redeemer of the world walked among men. There was uncontrolled hate and evil in the human heart. Satan personally did his utmost to turn Jesus aside from His purpose, and his legions entered into many people just as they do today to drive us into illness, paroxysms, and insanity.

Mary became an active follower of Jesus and gave generously of her wealth to supply the everyday needs of Jesus and His disciples. She became as passionately thankful realizing that at one time she was desperately ill. She was happiest in the Lord's company, marveling at the miracles, feeling the pulse beat with pity of the sheep without a shepherd . . . she walked proudly and unafraid with her Lord.

Mary had been aghast at Salome's request for honor on their last journey (Mark 15:41) together from Galilee to Jerusalem. All Mary wanted was to be near Jesus, because she loved Him. He had done so much for her that she wanted to give every moment of her redeemed life to serve Him. At the end of the journey, she walked with her Lord into Jerusalem, where the Lamb of God was to be made an offering for sin. Mary and John shared their love and adoration for the Master. In the Palace of the High Priest, watching the meek and lowly One suffering the indignities of a sham trial at the injustice of an enemy of the law, of false claims to equality with God, to Kingship. Mary's loyalty knew no bounds. Even though all the disciples, but one, had hidden in terror, she and the other women followed the cross with the hissing mob through the appointed gate to Golgotha. In the fringe of the crowd, the women huddled (Matthew 27:55-56). Shaking and with sobs, they cringed at each hammer blow, and as the cross lodged with a thud in the ground, Mary and two of the women edged among the soldiers and mockers to the foot of the cross. Her spirit and love for Jesus were so strong that she felt better standing to see His anguish than being separated from Him.

Mary saw everything—the soldiers with their high helmets and heavy spears, joking as they cast lots for the Savior's robe; the leers and jibes. She shuddered when the thieves mocked Him from their places on the conspicuous hill of death. (Matthew 27:41-44). When the Savior dismissed his mother (John 19:26-27), he kept Mary. He did not dismiss her nor would she go away. She was not afraid of the darkness for she was near the Lord of her life. His every word was indelibly written on her heart. He bowed His head; she saw Him die; but she would not leave even His dead body. While Joseph of Arimathaea went to ask Pilate for permission to take down the body of Jesus and Nicodemus went to buy spices, Mary waited by the cross, and release and washed the bloody body of the Savior. Sadly, she followed to the grave and watched intently as the men laid Jesus on a bed of spices. She may have helped wrap His body in clean linen. All this had to be done in a hurry because there were only about three hours left before the Sabbath. Mary was not satisfied and came back on the Sabbath day to finish the task. Mary was so reluctant to leave even His dead body (Matthew 27:61). Not for a moment could she forget Jesus, and early the next morning, while it was still dark, she went to the tomb with a few other women. In eagerness, she hurried ahead and, as she was last at the cross and she became the first to see the empty tomb and to witness the resurrection (Mark 16:9; John 20:1).

When she saw the empty tomb, she ran to get Peter and John and came back with them. The men saw that the body was gone and ran to tell the other disciples. But Mary, disturbed that His precious body was spirited away, stood alone beside the grave weeping. Then once more she stopped to look in, God made a rainbow of her tears, she saw two angels in brilliant white, and one of them said, "Woman, why weepest thou?" She turned away and there in the garden, by the grave astonished, that could not the resurrected Lord showing Himself to her first of all. And the word He said to her was, "Woman." Who can fathom the love and tenderness of Jesus when He said, "Mary." What relief, what amazement in Mary's response, "Master!" In her excitement, she rushed to embrace His feet as if to keep Him forever with her (John 20:17).

ACTION STEPS:

* Seek God so you may know how to give Him glory in your worship and praise at all times.
* God is more than willing to pour out His heart and thoughts to you.

THOUGHT FOR THE DAY:

Do not fill as if you have to remain silent about your love for Jesus Christ and the Word of God.

PRAYER:

Lord, You are my refuge and my strength, a very present help in times of trouble. You for your Word which guide and sustained me in the dark hours when it seemed my faith would fail. May I continue to hide your Word in my heart against the difficult days ahead. In the name of Jesus, I pray. Amen.

PROVERBS 29

1. He, that being often reproved hardeneth his neck, shall suddenly be destroyed, and that without remedy.
2. When the righteous are in authority, the people rejoice: but when the wicked beareth rule, the people mourn.
3. Whoso loveth wisdom rejoiceth his father: but he that keepeth company with harlots spendeth his substance.
4. The king by judgment establisheth the land: but he that receiveth gifts overthroweth it.
5. A man that flattereth his neighbour spreadeth a net for his feet.
6. In the transgression of an evil man there is a snare: but the righteous doth sing and rejoice.
7. The righteous considereth the cause of the poor: but the wicked regardeth not to know it.
8. Scornful men bring a city into a snare: but wise men turn away wrath.
9. If a wise man contendeth with a foolish man, whether he rage or laugh, there is no rest.
10. The bloodthirsty hate the upright: but the just seek his soul.
11. A fool uttereth all his mind: but a wise man keepeth it in till afterwards.
12. If a ruler hearken to lies, all his servants are wicked.
13. The poor and the deceitful man meet together: the LORD lighteneth both their eyes.
14. The king that faithfully judgeth the poor, his throne shall be established for ever.
15. The rod and reproof give wisdom: but a child left to himself bringeth his mother to shame.

16. *When the wicked are multiplied, transgression increaseth: but the righteous shall see their fall.*
17. *Correct thy son, and he shall give thee rest; yea, he shall give delight unto thy soul.*
18. *Where there is no vision, the people perish: but he that keepeth the law, happy is he.*
19. *A servant will not be corrected by words: for though he understand he will not answer.*
20. *Seest thou a man that is hasty in his words? there is more hope of a fool than of him.*
21. *He that delicately bringeth up his servant from a child shall have him become his son at the length.*
22. *An angry man stirreth up strife, and a furious man aboundeth in transgression.*
23. *A man's pride shall bring him low: but honour shall uphold the humble in spirit.*
24. *Whoso is partner with a thief hateth his own soul: he heareth cursing, and bewrayeth it not.*
25. *The fear of man bringeth a snare: but whoso putteth his trust in the LORD shall be safe.*
26. *Many seek the ruler's favour; but every man's judgment cometh from the LORD.*
27. *An unjust man is an abomination to the just: and he that is upright in the way is abomination to the wicked.*

Chapter 29

DON'T BE LIKE JEZEBEL'S TRAGEDY

> When the wicked are multiplied, transgression increaseth: but the righteous shall see their fall.
>
> **Proverbs 29:16**

Jezebel was the daughter of the king of Sidon and was totally committed to the virulent form of Baal worship practiced there. Her marriage to Ahab resulted in Ahab worshiping the Sidonian deity and cooperating with Jezebel in her efforts to make Baal the god of Israel. She came close to succeeding (1 Kings 18:4, 13), these verses make it clear that Jezebel took initiative in the religious crusade. Jezebel killed the prophets of the Lord at her command. This and other references to Jezebel in the Old Testament make it clear that she was a forceful woman. In many ways, Jezebel dominated her husband and set the course of the kingdom. God responded to Jezebel's threat by raising Elijah. Elijah not only turned the hearts of the people back to the Lord, but he predicted Jezebel's death as a punishment from God. In the end, God commissioned an army officer named Jehu to replace Ahab. Jehu fulfilled God's commission by wiping out all those in Israel who worshiped Baal and by killing every member of Ahab's household.

Jezebel was a determined opponent of God, set on wiping out His prophets and purging Israel of worshipers of the Lord. She initiated a campaign to exterminate God's prophets and threatened Elijah's life. Despite her antagonism toward the Lord, it seems significant that when Elijah challenged the 450 prophets of Baal and the four hundred prophets of Asherah (Baal's consort goddess) who eat at Jezebel's table to a contest, king Ahab accepted the challenge. However, Jezebel did not permit her prophets to enter the fray. Jezebel's antagonism to God may not have been rooted in disbelief as much as in a rejection of the moral standards for which the Lord stood.

Jezebel exercised dominance over her royal husband. This was striking because Ahab was a skilled military man and a capable ruler. Twice he defeated the forces of Syria's king Benhadad II. Ahab also joined a coalition of kings that defeated the Assyrians under Shalmaneser II at Qarqar in 853 B.C., contributing more war chariots to the allied effort than any other ruler. Ahab also maintained peace with Judah, working out an alliance with king Jehoshaphat. Yet the biblical text suggests that his wife, Jezebel dominated Ahab.

It was only natural that Jezebel's antagonism with the Lord would make her the enemy of Elijah, God's prophet. When Elijah had defeated the prophets of Baal in a contest at Mount Carmel (1 Kings 18) and had 450 prophets of the pagan deity put to death, Ahab seemed subdued and quiet. But when Jezebel heard, her immediate reaction was to threaten to kill Elijah! And this time it was Elijah who broke, and "arose and ran for his life" (1 Kings 19:3). In the end, God restored Elijah's courage, and he was the one who announced concerning Jezebel, the Lord had spoke saying, "The dogs shall eat Jezebel by the wall of Jezreel"

(1 Kings 21:23). This is a testimony of the reality of God's power and His words that Elijah spoke, rather than Jezebel's threats.

The only reference about Jezebel in the New Testament is found in Revelation 2:20: "You allow that woman Jezebel, who calls herself a prophetess, to teach and seduce My servants to commit sexual immorality and eat things sacrificed to idols." Jezebel undoubtedly was a strong woman. She relied on her sexuality and the force of her character to dominate her husband, king Ahab and set national religious policy. The tragedy of Jezebel is that she committed to evil rather than to God.

ACTION STEPS:

* Don't continue to be an opponent of God's Word, set on wiping out the preacher He has placed over your soul to walk in oneness with the Word of God.
* God is more than willing to pour out His heart, His thoughts, and His ways to you.

THOUGHT FOR THE DAY:

Ask God to fill you with His holy spirit, so you can learn to keep harmony in your Christian walk and touch others with the love of Jesus Christ.

PRAYER:

Lord, fill me with your love and holy spirit so I can walk in harmony for your glory and strengthen me so I don't forsake seeking the Word of God to learn of your Word, Ways, and Wisdom. In the name of Jesus, I pray. Amen.

PROVERBS 30

1. *The words of Agur the son of Jakeh, even the prophecy: the man spake unto Ithiel, even unto Ithiel and Ucal,*
2. *Surely I am more brutish than any man, and have not the understanding of a man.*
3. *I neither learned wisdom, nor have the knowledge of the holy.*
4. *Who hath ascended up into heaven, or descended? who hath gathered the wind in his fists? who hath bound the waters in a garment? who hath established all the ends of the earth? what is his name, and what is his son's name, if thou canst tell?*
5. *Every word of God is pure: he is a shield unto them that put their trust in him.*
6. *Add thou not unto his words, lest he reprove thee, and thou be found a liar.*
7. *Two things have I required of thee; deny me them not before I die:*
8. *Remove far from me vanity and lies: give me neither poverty nor riches; feed me with food convenient for me:*
9. *Lest I be full, and deny thee, and say, Who is the LORD? or lest I be poor, and steal, and take the name of my God in vain.*
10. *Accuse not a servant unto his master, lest he curse thee, and thou be found guilty.*
11. *There is a generation that curseth their father, and doth not bless their mother.*
12. *There is a generation that are pure in their own eyes, and yet is not washed from their filthiness.*
13. *There is a generation, O how lofty are their eyes! and their eyelids are lifted up.*

14. *There is a generation, whose teeth are as swords, and their jaw teeth as knives, to devour the poor from off the earth, and the needy from among men.*
15. *The horseleach hath two daughters, crying, Give, give. There are three things that are never satisfied, yea, four things say not, It is enough:*
16. *The grave; and the barren womb; the earth that is not filled with water; and the fire that saith not, It is enough.*
17. *The eye that mocketh at his father, and despiseth to obey his mother, the ravens of the valley shall pick it out, and the young eagles shall eat it.*
18. *There be three things which are too wonderful for me, yea, four which I know not:*
19. *The way of an eagle in the air; the way of a serpent upon a rock; the way of a ship in the midst of the sea; and the way of a man with a maid.*
20. *Such is the way of an adulterous woman; she eateth, and wipeth her mouth, and saith, I have done no wickedness.*
21. *For three things the earth is disquieted, and for four which it cannot bear:*
22. *For a servant when he reigneth; and a fool when he is filled with meat;*
23. *For an odious woman when she is married; and an handmaid that is heir to her mistress.*
24. *There be four things which are little upon the earth, but they are exceeding wise:*
25. *The ants are a people not strong, yet they prepare their meat in the summer;*
26. *The conies are but a feeble folk, yet make they their houses in the rocks;*
27. *The locusts have no king, yet go they forth all of them by bands;*
28. *The spider taketh hold with her hands, and is in kings' palaces.*

29. *There be three things which go well, yea, four are comely in going:*
30. *A lion which is strongest among beasts, and turneth not away for any;*
31. *A greyhound; an he goat also; and a king, against whom there is no rising up.*
32. *If thou hast done foolishly in lifting up thyself, or if thou hast thought evil, lay thine hand upon thy mouth.*
33. *Surely the churning of milk bringeth forth butter, and the wringing of the nose bringeth forth blood: so the forcing of wrath bringeth forth strife.*

Chapter 30

ARE YOU MODELING YOUR RUBIES

There is a generation that curseth their father, and doth not bless their mother.

Proverbs 30:11

Women, you must remember that God has placed in you all the characters of a Proverb 31st Woman. You just have to decide to walk in Him. Remember that your words can change a day. In the course of life, you can instill confidence into your children's hearts, you can encourage your husband to accomplish his dreams. You can draw someone to the love of Jesus Christ. You can't read very far in the New Testament without realizing that love is important to God. He calls us women who love God...

- To walk in love   (Ephesians 5:2)
- To love one another   (John 15:12)
- To love our husbands and our children   (Titus 2:4)
- To love our neighbor   (Matthew 27:39)
- To love our enemies   (Luke 6:27)

As children of God, you and I are commanded to show forth the kind of love that has been modeled by our heavenly Father and His Son Jesus Christ.

Proverbs 31 - Shows us the only ideal description of a wife within the Bible. Even as a single woman, you must remember that you are the bride of Christ, so your character must be molded to line up with Jesus Christ as your husbandman, so His light may be a model for others to see.

What a rare find is a capable wife! Her worth is far beyond that of rubies.

Her husband puts his confidence in her. And lacks no good thing.

She is good to him, never bad. All the days of her life.

She looks for wood and flax. And set her hand to them with a will.

She is like a merchant fleet. bringing her food from afar.

She rises while it is still night. And supplies provisions for her household.

The daily fare of her maids. She sets her mind on an estate and acquires it; she plants a vineyard through her labors. She girds herself with strength.

And performs her tasks with vigor. She sees that her business thrives; her lamp never goes out at night. She sets her hand to the distaff; her fingers work the spindle. She gives generously to the poor;

Her hands are stretched out to the needy. She is not worried for her household because of the snow. For her whole household is dressed in crimson.

She makes covers for herself; Her clothing is lined and purple.

Her husband is prominent at the gates. As he sits among the elders of the land.

She makes clothes and sells them. And offers a girdle to the merchant, she is clothed with strength and splendor; she looks to the future cheerfully.

Her mouth is full of wisdom. Her tongue with kindly teaching.

She oversees the activities of her household. And never eats the bread of idleness.

Her children declare her happy; her husband praises her.

"Many women have done well, but you surpass them all!"

Grace is deceptive. Beauty is illusory; It is for her fear of the Lord That a woman is to be praised. Extol her for the fruit of her hand.

And let her works praise her in the gates.

ACTION STEPS:

* Seek God to help you with His direction so your character can line up to model a Proverbs 31st Woman.
* Remember that God has placed in you as a believer His character to model a Proverbs 31st Woman.

THOUGHT FOR THE DAY:

Ask God to give you His patience and wisdom on how to become a Proverb 31st Woman, so you can model His love.

PRAYER:

Lord, teach me how to become a Proverbs 31st Woman and to wait patiently in faith. In the name of Jesus, I pray. Amen.

PROVERBS 31

1. The words of king Lemuel, the prophecy that his mother taught him.
2. What, my son? and what, the son of my womb? and what, the son of my vows?
3. Give not thy strength unto women, nor thy ways to that which destroyeth kings.
4. It is not for kings, O Lemuel, it is not for kings to drink wine; nor for princes strong drink:
5. Lest they drink, and forget the law, and pervert the judgment of any of the afflicted.
6. Give strong drink unto him that is ready to perish, and wine unto those that be of heavy hearts.
7. Let him drink, and forget his poverty, and remember his misery no more.
8. Open thy mouth for the dumb in the cause of all such as are appointed to destruction.
9. Open thy mouth, judge righteously, and plead the cause of the poor and needy.
10. Who can find a virtuous woman? for her price is far above rubies.
11. The heart of her husband doth safely trust in her, so that he shall have no need of spoil.
12. She will do him good and not evil all the days of her life.
13. She seeketh wool, and flax, and worketh willingly with her hands.
14. She is like the merchants' ships; she bringeth her food from afar.
15. She riseth also while it is yet night, and giveth meat to her household, and a portion to her maidens.

16. *She considereth a field, and buyeth it: with the fruit of her hands she planteth a vineyard.*
17. *She girdeth her loins with strength, and strengtheneth her arms.*
18. *She perceiveth that her merchandise is good: her candle goeth not out by night.*
19. *She layeth her hands to the spindle, and her hands hold the distaff.*
20. *She stretcheth out her hand to the poor; yea, she reacheth forth her hands to the needy.*
21. *She is not afraid of the snow for her household: for all her household are clothed with scarlet.*
22. *She maketh herself coverings of tapestry; her clothing is silk and purple.*
23. *Her husband is known in the gates, when he sitteth among the elders of the land.*
24. *She maketh fine linen, and selleth it; and delivereth girdles unto the merchant.*
25. *Strength and honour are her clothing; and she shall rejoice in time to come.*
26. *She openeth her mouth with wisdom; and in her tongue is the law of kindness.*
27. *She looketh well to the ways of her household, and eateth not the bread of idleness.*
28. *Her children arise up, and call her blessed; her husband also, and he praiseth her.*
29. *Many daughters have done virtuously, but thou excellest them all.*
30. *Favour is deceitful, and beauty is vain: but a woman that feareth the LORD, she shall be praised.*
31. *Give her of the fruit of her hands; and let her own works praise her in the gates.*

Chapter 31

LASTING INFLUENCES OF A NOBLE CHARACTER

Who can find a virtuous woman? for her price is far above rubies.

Proverbs 31:10

One of the women that comes to my mind as having a noble character and was far more than rubies was mother Geneva Hutchins. Mother Hutchins lived in Dacula, Georgia. In her early childhood, she accepted Jesus Christ. As a young child, she attended the Buford Public Schools system and after high school, she attended DeKalb Technical Schools of nursing where she obtained her license in practical nursing. In 1943, Geneva married Clifford Hutchins and to their union were five children born, seven grandchildren, six great-grandchildren, and a host of nieces, and nephews. Mother Hutchins during her nursing career gave birth to almost every child that was born within the Lawrenceville, Dacula, and Buford area, she was also their community nurse, and she touched the lives of those who were not born within her community. After she retired from the hospital, she would still work so hard in her community and clean her church. After her husband passed, she also took care of her lawn and yard work, cutting weeds and trimming bushes. Her saying was "I may wear out, but I will never rust out." Mother Hutchins always ministered to the younger ladies about keeping peace in their homes and not being a busybody.

I met her and truly got to know her as one of the church mothers and one day I ran across a poem she wrote, so I went to visit her to get her permission to incorporate it within the first book that I wrote, later, I learned that she had five children, two sons, and three daughters and all of them loved and cherished mother Hutchins so much that every Sunday they still had dinner with her even though they were adults and had families of their own. All of the children, grandchildren, and great-grandchildren, always celebrate all of her birthdays with her in a grand way. She and I became so close over the years that when I met my husband, he asked me to marry him, being that my mother lived up north. I took him to meet mother Hutchins. Before I gave him an answer that I would marry him, I wanted a woman of wisdom, and noble character to give me her input into the matters, and relationships of my future.

A Kind Word

A kind word costs but little but may bless the one to whom it is spoken all through the day. Have not kind words been spoken to you that have lived in your heart through the years and have borne fruit of joy and hope? Let us speak kindly to one another. We have burdens and worries, but let us not on that account rasp and irritate those near us. Speak kindly at night for before dawn some loved one may finish his or her span of life in this world and tomorrow will be too late to ask for forgiveness.

By: Mrs. Geneva Hutchins

Proverbs 31 "virtuous woman" got in on that teaching. She could laugh at the days to come. Even when her future held flabby abs and combustible thighs too. Why? Because the passage describes a woman who seems just about perfect. Many Bible teachers call her the "virtuous woman" and she makes Martha Stewart look like a beginner. She kept her husband happy; she works eagerly; she got up early and stayed up late. She gave to others generously, and her children love her. She was a formidable pattern, and an intimidating example for other women to follow.

As you looked past the outer layer and deeper, you could see a woman of wisdom who fully understood what was important. She understood what it meant to work hard and to serve God with her whole heart. She understood that everything of consequence was wrapped up in Him. Serving others came as a natural extension of serving Him. This picture keeps every woman eternally beautiful because it's a matter of the heart. The Scripture says, "Therefore, if anyone is in Christ, he is a new creation; the old has gone, the new has come!" (2 Corinthians 5:17). Having a heart of unselfish service that has been transformed by Christ—that's what's important.

Mother Hutchins loved to praise and serve the Lord with all of her heart, soul, and mind, she was working her crossword puzzles up until the time the Lord called her home, and all of her children wore purple to honor her at the home-going celebration.

On September 4th, God strolled through His flower garden on His daily run while the dew was still on the roses, He picked each perfect flower He came upon. Later that afternoon His bouquet was nearly complete, needing only one more perfect flower. He whispered softly in her ear, Geneva, my child, this is your hour. The most perfect rose, it's you that I chose. We must hurry along and not be late, your husband Clifford, awaits you at the gate. Mother, your pain and suffering are finally over for you are now coming to rest at Jesus' feet. Mother Hutchins, we forever miss you and love you, but God loves you best. So go with Him for He'll give you rest.

ACTION STEPS:

- Remember God's wisdom so you may know how to give Him glory.
- God is more than willing to pour out His heart to help you learn His character.
- Walk in a way that younger people seek Godly wisdom and standards from you.

THOUGHT FOR THE DAY:

Ask God to fill you with His harmony in your Christian walk so you can touch others with the love of Jesus Christ.

PRAYER:

Lord, fill me with your love and holy spirit so I can walk in harmony for your glory and strengthen me so I don't forsake seeking the Word of God to learn of your Word, Ways, and Wisdom. In the name of Jesus, I pray. Amen.

Lifting your Husband through Prayer

Praying for Your Husband

A wise woman prays for her husband. She begins before she is married before she even knows him, and she continues for the rest of her life. No other person is more central or more important in your life—and he always needs your prayers, even though he may not always tell you so.

If you're going to pray for your husband, you've got to know what's going on in his life, what he's doing, what he's thinking, what he's feeling... A wise wife will make it a top priority to be with her husband and talk to him. As the years go by, she will learn to read him and to see beneath the surface.

Praying for Yourself as a Wife

Ask yourself: What does my husband need in a wife? What things does he need from me? What qualities does he need to see exhibited in my life? Then pray that God will begin developing these qualities in you.

The following prayer is one I pray for my husband:

Father in heaven, help me to be the woman my husband needs me to be today. I know that I cannot meet his every need, only You can do that, but help me to always be caring and attentive toward him. Help me to be sensitive to his concerns and to provide for him as I ought. Enable me to listen to what he says, and to always be courteous and thoughtful toward him and encouraging to him in all his efforts. Help me always to be alert, to defend him against harm or insult. Please give me the will and energy to share my heart and my thoughts with him, and to tell him the things that seem self-evident to me but may not be clear to him at all. Help me to be kind, appreciative, and fun to live with. Amen.

"Following Jesus' pattern of intercession in John 17, . . . A wife should pray for her husband that . . ."

- God would be glorified in and through his life.
- He would know God and grow in knowledge and experience of Him.
- God would keep him safe in Him (protect him from despair, discouragement, and faithlessness amid trials).
- He would be morally pure and set apart for His service.
- He would be one with God, with his wife, and be a pure brother to the women in the body of Christ.
- He would stay faithful to Christ to the end.

I WORSHIP YOU FOR WHO YOU ARE!!!

Lord how excellent is thy name in all the Earth. There is none like you.

You are Yahweh	—Lord Jehovah Psalm 102:27
You are Adonai	—Master Exodus 21:1-6
You are El Shaddai	—All Sufficient One Genesis 17:18
You are the Father of Jesus Christ	—Abba Father Mark 14:36
You are Jehovah Jireh	—The God who provides Genesis 22:1-2
You are Jehovah Nissi	—The God my banner Exodus 17:15
You are Jehovah Shalom	—God of Peace Judge 6:21-24
You are Jehovah Shammah	—The Lord is there Genesis 3:8
You are Jehovah Tsidkenou	—Righteousness Jeremiah 23:5-6
You are Jehovah Rohi	—The God My Shepherd Psalm 23
You are El Elyon	—The God most High Genesis 14:18
You are Jehovah Elohay	—The Lord is my God 1 Peter 4:12
You are El Elohe-Israel	—The personal God of Israel Genesis 32:11
You are Jehovah Eloheenu	—The Lord our God Exodus 32:3-5
You are Love, Joy, Peace, and Faithful	—Galatians 5:22-26

You are Jehovah M'Kaddesh —You are the Jehovah who Sanctifies Lev. 20:7-8

You are Elohim —Creator of all things in the heavens and in the earth Genesis 1:1-2

You are Jehovah Makkeh —The Lord our smiter, perfecting us into smooth lively stones Psalm 51:17

You are Omnipotent, Omnipresent, and Omniscient

You are the Alpha and the Omega—the Beginning and the end

You are the Way, the Truth, and the Life —John 14:6

You are the Bridge over troubled waters

You are the God of Abraham, Isaac, and Jacob

You are the I Am That I Am

THE OPTION IS YOURS!

The day finally came, and one by one we were called
To stand before God in the great judgment hall.
The books were all opened and our record was there;
It was too late to be sorry and no time for prayer.

As I stood before Him and looked in His face,
My life came before me and what a disgrace.
I had spent my life fulfilling all my desires,
I had my heaven and earth—I didn't fear Hell's fires.

He looked into my eyes and He said to me,
Did it occur to you there is an eternity?
I gave you a talent. You never used it for me,
You only used your talent—a living to make;
Earth's glitter and gleam made your soul forsake me.

He said, "My child—didn't you know that all the gold is mine;
The cattle, the hills, and I even own time.
You could have served me without sin in your life;
Enjoying all my peace with health and no strife.

My Son came to earth for this story to tell,
He told you about the pay days of Heaven and Hell.
He made a way of escape from a life of sin;
He left the door open for you to come in.

But you slammed the door in My Son's face,
Now you stand before Me in this hollowed place.
You chose the place, while you lived on earth,
The option was yours, from the day of birth."

> You must accept God as your Lord and Savior in order to achieve Salvation.
>
> Need proof? Maybe an interview? Well, here's a copy of His resume.
>
> He is the only qualified candidate for the job.

Dear Friend:

I heard you were considering a new manager for your life. I would like to apply for the job. I believe I am the most qualified candidate. I am the only one that has ever done this job successfully. I was the first manager of human beings. In fact, I created them. So naturally, I know how humanity works and what is best to get people back into proper working conditions. It will be like having the manufacturer as your personal mechanic.

If this is your first time considering Me, I would just like to point out that My Salary has already been paid by the Blood of My Son, Jesus Christ, on the cross of Calvary. What I need from you is the acknowledgment that the price is sufficient to pay for all of your sins and your independence from Me. I need you to believe this in your heart and to tell somebody else about your decision with your mouth.

The next thing I ask is the right to change and fix your life so you learn how to stay close to Me. I will make some major changes and revisions. They are not for you to worry about, I need your permission to execute these changes My Way and in My Time, I will change your desires and give you the strength to make the changes. Please keep your hands out of the way. Don't try to help Me, and don't resist Me. I do need your commitment and cooperation. If you give Me those, the process can go smoothly without delays.

Your Sincerely,

GOD

P.S. I Am. I Can and I Will. I Created the Heavens and Earth.

God's Beatitudes
Matthew 5

Blessed are the poor in spirit
for theirs is the kingdom of heaven.

Blessed are they that mourn,
for they shall be comforted.
Blessed are the meek,
for they shall inherit the earth.

Blessed are they which do hunger and thirst after righteousness,
for they shall be filled.

Blessed are the merciful,
for they shall obtain mercy.

Blessed are the pure in heart,
for they shall see God.
Blessed are the peacemakers,
for they shall be called the children of God.

Blessed are they which are persecuted for righteousness' sake,
for theirs is the kingdom of heaven.
Blessed are you, when men shall insult you, persecute you, and shall say
all manner of evil against you falsely, for My sake.

Rejoice, and be exceeding glad: for great is your reward in heaven,
for in the same way they persecuted the prophets which were before you.

A Letter from Satan

This is just a letter of appreciation from me to you. I'd like to say "Thanks" for letting me use you for most of your life. You are so gullible, I saw you yesterday as you began your daily chores, you awoke without praying. As a matter of fact, you didn't even bless your meals or pray before going to bed last night. You are so unthankful I like that about you.

I cannot tell you how glad I am that you decided to go another day without giving your life and your will to God. I am so glad that you have not changed your way of living. You are mine. Remember, you and I have been going steady for years, and I don't love you yet. As a matter of fact, I HATE YOU! I hate you because I hate God, I'm only using you to get even with God. He kicked me out of heaven down to this earth and I'm going to make your life a living hell. That way, we'll be together twice.

This will really hurt God. Thanks to you, I'm really showing Him who's boss in your life. With all the good times we have had to watching dirty movies, cussing folks out, partying, stealing, lying, being used as a hypocrite, fornicating, smoking, drinking, working roots, telling dirty jokes, gossiping, and backstabbing other folks. Come on, lets' burn together forever. I've got some hot plans for us.

Well, I've gotta go now. I'll be back in a few second to tempt you again. If you were smart, you would run somewhere, confess your sins, and live for God with what little bit of life you have left. It's not my nature to warn anyone. But to be your age and still sinning is becoming a bit ridiculous.

If you really love me, you will keep doing the things in my letter and you will not share this information with others, so they can keep servicing me.

Sincerely,

Satan

Satan's Beatitudes

Blessed are those who are too tired, too busy, and too distracted to spend an hour once a week with their fellow Christians in Church
They are my best workers.

Blessed are those Christians who wait to be asked and expect to be thanked
I can use them.

Blessed are the touchy people, with a bit of luck they may stop going to church
They are my missionaries.

Blessed are those very religious people who get on everybody else nerves
They are mine forever.

Blessed are the troublemakers with church
They shall be called my children.

Blessed are those who have no time to pray
They are very easy prey for me.

Blessed are the Church's gossip
For they are my secret agents.

Blessed are those who are critical of the Church leadership
For they shall inherit a place with me in my fate.

Blessed are the complainers
I'm all ears for them.

Blessed are you when you read this and think it is about other people and not yourself
I've got you.

Women

What makes me weak?	*My fears . . . .*
What makes me whole?	*My religion.*
What keeps me standing?	*My faith.*
What empowers me?	*My spirit.*
What helps me know I need love?	*God opening my heart.*
What makes me victorious?	*My courage to climb.*
What makes me compassionate?	*My selflessness.*
What makes me honest?	*My integrity.*
What sustains my mind?	*My quest for knowledge.*
What teaches me all lessons?	*My past mistakes.*
What lift's my head high?	*My pride, not humility.*
What if I can't go on?	*Not an option.*
What makes me beautiful?	*My essence of God's everything.*
What makes me a woman of God?	*My heart truly loving God.*

The Four Different Personality Styles

Dominance Personality Style	This person tends to want results immediately and act decisively. They are determined and assertive, they are assertive in meeting their needs through the direction of others. Their style of personality can range from being more positive to negative behavior which may be described as "Decisive" at one end and "Defiant" at the other extreme.
Motivation	They feel they need personal control through a direct style.
Fear	They have a fear of being taken advantage of by others.
Effectiveness	This style tends to be oriented, forceful, and practical. When less effective, this style is likely to be seen as overbearing, insensitive, and distrustful. Increase effectiveness by developing further patience through accepting themselves and others. Even the limitations each of us possess as part of our human nature.
Influencing Personality Style	This person tends to want contact with people and act passionately. Their **Personality** influencing style tends to be entertaining and motivates them to interact with others. They are people-focused. This can range from being

"Invigorating" to "Impulsive and Indiscriminate" as negatively motivated or distressed.

Motivation	They feel they need personal approval from others through a direct style.
Fear	They have a fear of loss of influence with others.
Effectiveness	This style tends to be influential, impulsive, and accessible to others. This style is likely to be excessive, extremely emotional, and superficial in its approach.
Steadiness Personality Style	This person tends to want stability and act systematically, their style tends to approach situations in a slower, more planned manner that is more likely to ensure actions and results. This can take the form of "Servicing" tendencies when positively motivated, and the other extreme is passive resistance through "Demanding" which holds onto what is already possessed and certain.
Motivation	They feel personal stability through an indirect style.
Fear	They have a fear of loss of stability such as predictable conditions, actions, and relationships in their environment.

Effectiveness	This style tends to be deliberate, objective, and consistent. When less effective, they're likely to be indecisive, over-systematic in their concern about all the details and procedures, and not expressive of their thoughts and feelings. Increase effectiveness by developing greater comfort and ability to deal with required change in situations, including growth in their own level of assertiveness.
Cautious Personality Style	This person tends to be precise, as reserved, and concerned with the appearance of conditions. This combines to explain their motivation by self-direction through an approach which tends to involve compliance to critical conditions, situations, individuals, and working relationships. This can lead to difficulties being resolved or otherwise controlled. They can range from being "Lost in Thought" and appearing courteous to being excessively "Critical" at their worst.
Motivation	Achieving their goals through an indirect style.
Fear	Criticism of their efforts and actions by others.

Effectiveness This style tends to be creative, inquisitive, and discrete. When less effective, this style is likely to be seen as a perfectionist, "Nitpicking," Overly-demanding of themselves and others, and detached or unfriendly. Increase the effectiveness by developing further acceptance of the realistic limitations on us. This is part of an attitude of increasing progress towards approximating the perfection which they desire to achieve.

www.ingramcontent.com/pod-product-compliance
Lightning Source LLC
LaVergne TN
LVHW040140080526
838202LV00042B/2972